THE
MIDDLE-SIZED
GARDEN

COMPLETE GUIDE TO GARDEN PRIVACY

BY ALEXANDRA CAMPBELL

www.themiddlesizedgarden.co.uk

THE MIDDLE-SIZED GARDEN

COMPLETE GUIDE TO GARDEN PRIVACY

ALEXANDRA CAMPBELL

DESIGNED AND ILLUSTRATED BY KARI BROWNLIE

ISBN 978 1 9163636 1 8

ACKNOWLEDGEMENTS

Design and illustration by Kari Brownlie
Thank you to David Iron for the diagrams

PHOTOGRAPHIC CREDITS

All photographs copyright Alexandra Campbell except for:

P24	fences reproduced by kind permission of Jacksons Fencing jacksons-fencing.co.uk
P33	Photo by Manuel T on Unsplash
P38	Photo by chuttersnap on Unsplash
P39	Photo by Thomas Millot on Unsplash
P48	Photo by Larisa Birta on Unsplash
P64	Photo by Sebastian Huxley on Unsplash
P74	Photo by Rod Long on Unsplash
P75	Photo by Annie Spratt on Unsplash
P77	Photo by Andrew Scherle on Unsplash
P78	Photo by Mahosadha Ong on Unsplash
P79	Photo by Carlita Benazito on Unsplash
P80	Photo by Francisco J. Villena on Unsplash
P83	Photo by Grant Durr on Unsplash
P84	Photo by Roman Kraft on Unsplash
P85	Photo by Jamie Street on Unsplash
P88	Photo by Alfred Lutz on Unsplash
P90	Photo by Diana Parkhouse on Unsplash
P95	Photo by Tim Foster on Unsplash
P102	Photo by Annie Spratt on Unsplash
P103	Photo by Luca N on Unsplash
P104	Photo by Tim Cooper on Unsplash

ABOUT
THE MIDDLESIZED GARDEN

The Middlesized Garden blog is one of the UK's leading gardening blogs, with tips, ideas and inspiration for people whose gardens are under an acre. It covers garden trends, interviews with expert gardeners and gardening tips. The Middlesized Garden on YouTube offers an opportunity to see more of the gardens featured on the Middlesized Garden blog, with expert interviews, garden tours, coverage of the top garden shows and more.

Connect with the Middlesized Garden on
Twitter @midsizegarden
Instagram @the_middlesized_garden_blog
Facebook @themiddlesizedgarden
http://www.youtube.com/c/ThemiddlesizedgardenCoUk

CONTENTS

INTRODUCTION

In today's crowded world, privacy is precious. And so is light. Do you have a neighbour's window looking down into your garden? Or do you see an ugly extension, street light or garage roof instead of your beautiful planting?

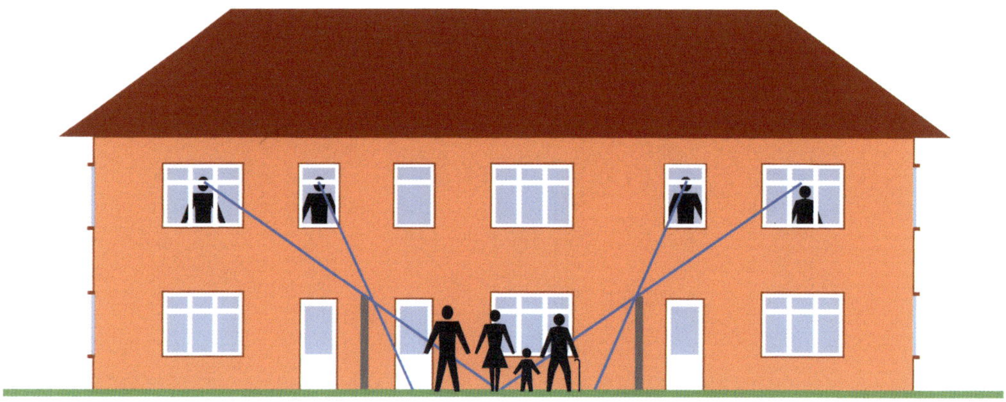

The Privacy Problem for a Terraced or Semi-Detached House

Perhaps you want to create a sanctuary within your garden – a private space or 'secret garden', where you can relax and feel that you are screened from the noise and busyness of day to day life?

This book will help you decide which screens, hedging, trees or fencing will help you achieve the garden you want.

Today's gardens and back yards are smaller on average than they have ever been. We all need ways of making our outdoor space our own.

In the past, garden privacy meant building a high wall, planting a tall tree or a high hedge. But high walls and rows of tall trees and hedges are not always practical – they may block your light or your neighbours' light. They are often ugly. And they may not be allowed under local regulations and by-laws.

Making your garden more private can also buffer sound if you use the right materials. Once again, it will be hard to make a city or town garden completely quiet, but a little muffling can help a great deal.

And if you use trees and shrubs, carefully placed and maintained, to increase your privacy and buffer sound, then you will also reduce pollution and help wildlife. Hedges and trees, in particular, offer shelter and food for garden birds. And trees absorb carbon dioxide and particle pollutants in the atmosphere.

And the right privacy screens, fences and planting can also reduce wind in your garden, so you can sit out even on blowy days.

This book will show you how to create beautiful, comfortable private spaces in your garden. At the end of each section, there is a space for your notes. When you're talking to friends or experts about your choices, you can make notes of their recommendations, usefully keeping all your research in one place.

CHAPTER 1
THE PRINCIPLES OF GARDEN PRIVACY

The first thing to ask yourself is 'Where do I want my privacy?'

In many of today's towns and cities – and even in the countryside – it's not always practical to make the whole garden private. But if you focus on where you really want to feel secluded, then you can enjoy your garden more.

Walk about your garden and decide where you really want to be private. Where would you like your seating area to be? Then look around and see who can overlook you when you're in that spot.

Or if you want to shield an eyesore, decide where you are most likely to spend time. Can you see the eyesore from there? If so, what is the line of sight that you need to interrupt?

And screening for privacy doesn't need to be ugly or overbearing. You can also make your garden look more attractive. Fences, screens, pergolas, gazebos or trellis can all be highly decorative as well as giving you privacy.

You can create a delightfully private 'secret garden' space even in the smallest garden by combining a trellis, screen, pergola and planting.

BOUNDARIES

When you're trying to make your garden private, think about your boundaries first. But remember they are not the only factors in how private your garden feels. Boundaries are fences, walls and hedges. You won't necessarily get the best results by simply making them as high as possible. But your choice of boundary and its height creates the starting point for all your other garden privacy solutions.

Boundaries are also where you're likely to encounter problems. Legislation or regulations often

A pop-up gazebo or tent can increase your privacy as well as provide shelter from the weather. There are tips on choosing a pop-up in chapter 6

govern the height of boundaries. And your neighbours may object if you make your boundaries too high – or too low! For example, you may want to make your garden feel lighter, but your neighbours may value their privacy more. Or the other way around.

Ideally, discuss any changes in the height of your boundaries with your neighbours before doing anything. Find out what their priorities are. And be aware that often people feel very threatened by any change in their boundaries – even if what you are planning seems so much better, your neighbours may still feel anxious about it. The more you can listen to their worries, the more likely you are to come up with a solution that everyone will feel happy about.

PRIMARY SPACE

It's important to make a difference between 'primary privacy space' and 'secondary privacy space'. Primary privacy space is the area where you want to achieve complete or almost-complete privacy. It could be where your garden table and chairs are, where you eat or where you want to place a deck chair or sun lounger. Perhaps you want a private area for a pool or outdoor jacuzzi, or you want to feel that your children can play safely without strangers watching them. Or there may be a window or windows in your house which are particularly overlooked.

Our diagrams will show you how to calculate the size of your primary space. If you want privacy when you eat outside, you need to feel that no neighbours or passers-by can see you when you are sitting at that table. Primary privacy can be achieved, often in the tiniest courtyard in the most crowded city.

Understanding where your primary privacy space is means that you can plant just one tree for maximum privacy or place a screen in exactly the right place so you can feel as private as possible. Our diagrams will show you exactly how high your tree, hedge, screen, fence or wall needs to be to give you privacy.

And the closer a screen, hedge, fence or wall is to your primary space, the lower it can be. A high hedge at the end of your garden gives you less privacy than a low screen near your eating area. So you can have privacy and light – and you're less likely to affect your neighbours' light.

See our diagram below.

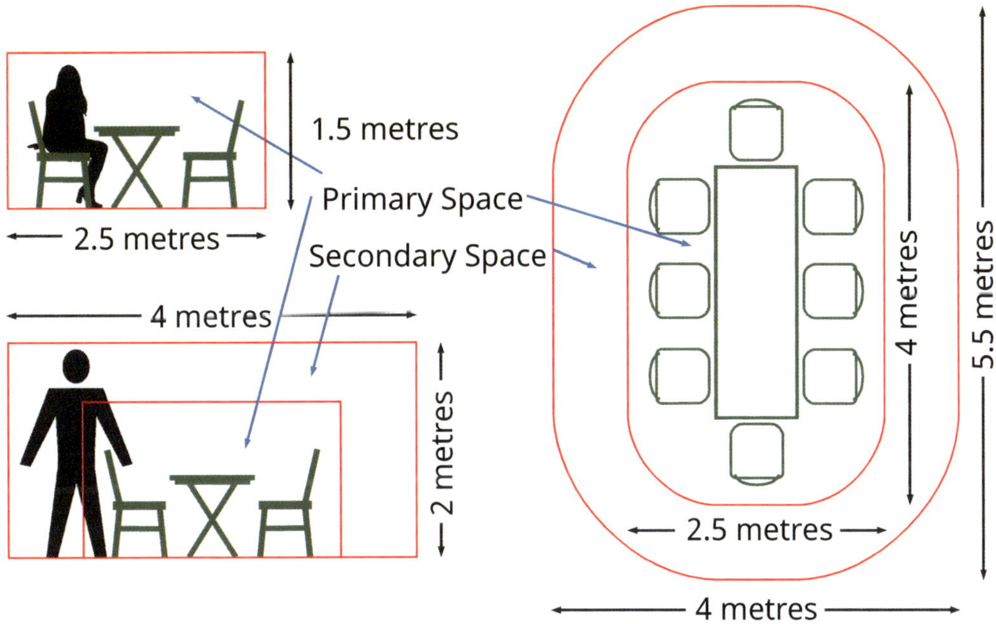

Primary & Secondary Privacy Spaces

And there are easy explanations for those who don't like diagrams. If you are sitting at a table in a part of your garden, then there's a good chance that you can make it private. It's less easy to be private if you are standing up or walking around the garden. However, you can often ensure that you can only be glimpsed in passing.

SECONDARY SPACE

This is what we call the area around your core space where you may also be able to achieve a degree of garden privacy.

For example, if your garden table and chairs are in a completely private spot, can you be seen briefly when you get up and walk round the table? And how much does that matter to you?

We call this 'secondary space.' The secondary space is larger than the primary space and it may be harder to achieve complete privacy – but if you think about it carefully, you can probably achieve more privacy than you might have otherwise expected. And you'll be able to make sure that it all looks good, too.

For example, you create a small private area at the bottom of your garden for a table and four chairs. When you're sitting down, enjoying a meal, you're completely private. When you get up and walk around the table, to refill your glass or turn over the burgers on the barbecue, then perhaps you could be spotted. That's the secondary area.

TARGETED PRIVACY

In many towns and cities, rows of houses and gardens back onto each other. You may have a window or windows overlooking your garden. But they can only see quite a limited view. In order to create privacy, all you need to do is interrupt that view. One tree placed in exactly the right part of your garden can interrupt the view from several windows – without making your garden look dark or crowded.

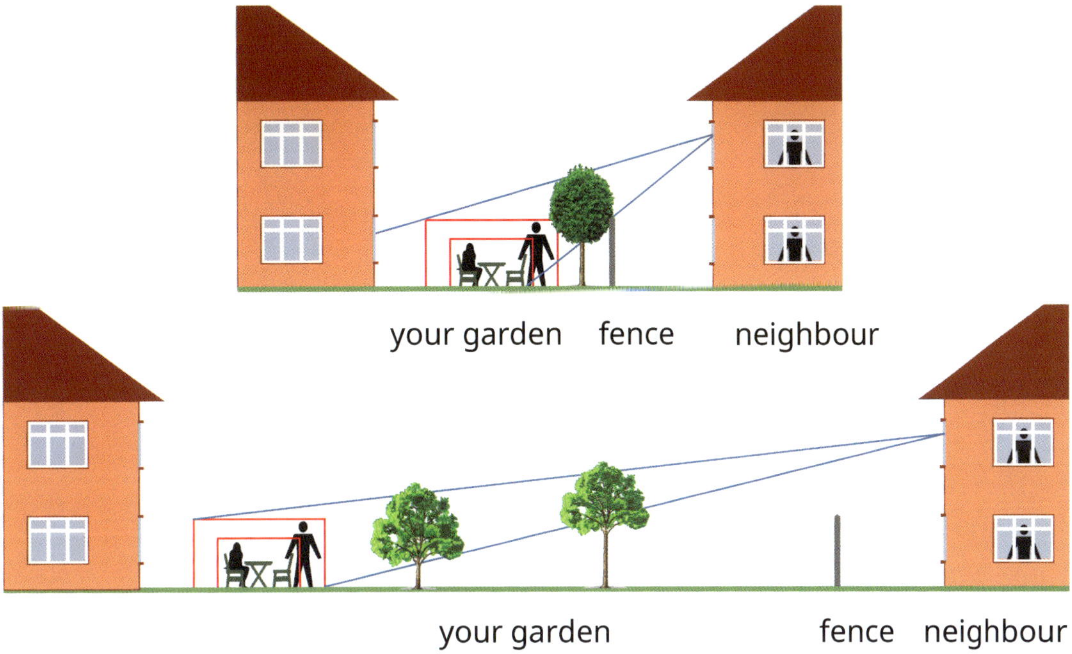

Proximity

In our chapter on Trees, we'll show you the different tree shapes and how to choose the right shape of tree – one that blocks only the sightline from the overlooking window, not all the light in the garden.

This broken screen distracts the eye. Look at the garden as a whole. Then focus on the tents you can see on the other side of the screen. When you're looking at the garden, you hardly notice them because the eye is distracted. Designed by Kate Gould.

DISTRACTING THE EYE

You don't always need to block out an eyesore completely. If you give the eye something interesting to look at, then the eye often doesn't notice the eyesore or overlooking window behind. When you're thinking about what privacy you want and why, it's worth considering whether distraction will serve you as well as any solid screen.

Distracting the eye can be more attractive and just as effective as creating a solid screen. An example of distraction is when trellis or a laser-cut screen creates a sense of privacy. If anyone was to press their eye to the gaps or holes, they could see you – but if the screen is inside your garden, they tend not to.

Tests have shown that planting

a geometric row of trees to screen an eyesore isn't as effective a distraction to the eye as planting one or two trees with different shapes and leaf colours around the space. People look at the distraction tree, because it is a beautiful shape or colour. They don't then notice the ugly eyesore beyond it.

But if you have a very geometric hedge then anything that disturbs that neatness, such as the roof of your neighbour's extension, will be quite obvious.

ALL YEAR OR SUMMER ONLY

If you want to be shielded from a window or a street lamp all year round, then you need either a solid screen, such as a wall or fence. Or you need evergreen trees or hedging.

However, if you spend much more time in the garden in the summer than the winter, then deciduous trees and hedging could be better, even though they lose their leaves in autumn. There is a greater choice of deciduous trees and shrubs. Many have beautiful spring flowers and stunning autumn colour, so they add interest to your garden as well as increasing your privacy.

Light levels are lower in the winter, too. So if you are thinking about the impact that a tree or hedge will have inside your house, you may wish to choose one which has no leaves in the winter so that the house is a little lighter during the short winter days.

And outside in the garden, you can create summer-only private spaces with perennial or deciduous plants. For example, a big border with tall plants makes a 'summer hedge'. You may be able to create a feeling of a 'secret garden' space just by using tall plants, such as grasses, without having to have permanent hedging or screening.

PULLING IT ALL TOGETHER

It can be very effective to combine two or three different ways of creating garden privacy. For example, an eating space may have a hedge on its boundary side, plus a pergola or canopy over the top. And perhaps you could plant a small, pretty tree a few feet away to interrupt the sight line from a window. The garden may be small and surrounded by windows, but combining three elements mean that no-one overlooks the seating area

YOUR NOTES

Make a rough diagram of where you want your privacy and what the sightlines are. Or what ugly feature you want to conceal.

WHAT ARE YOU ALLOWED TO DO?

Many countries, districts, towns, villages and developments have regulations on how high hedges, fences, walls, screens and garden buildings can be. High hedges, for example, are covered by national legislation in Britain. And when housing developments are built, there are often some extra local regulations which will affect how you manage your privacy.

It is your responsibility to find out what legislation and regulations could affect your plans for creating more privacy in your garden. You may need planning permission for some structures and there may be height restrictions on others. Your local planning department will have the details on their websites or should be able to help you in person.

When you find out what the regulations are, you may look at your local streets and see that many people are not complying. In Britain, for example, you need planning permission for a front garden hedge, wall or fence more than 1 metre high (3ft 3"). Yet when you walk down a road in any British town or village, you will see that many front hedges, walls and fences are obviously higher than one metre. It's unlikely that they all applied for planning permission.

However, that doesn't give you the right to flout the regulations yourself. You may decide that you'll take the risk and hope that no-one complains. But someone may complain – especially if you live on the corner of two roads and your higher hedge or fence means that cars can't emerge safely from a junction.

Find out what regulations or legislation apply to you, and then re-visit our diagrams showing how to maximise your privacy. A low screen or hedge near your table or window can give you much more privacy than a higher one further away. Our diagrams will show you how to position your tree, hedge or screen so that you get the maximum privacy with the lowest possible screen.

In this book, we will give examples based on UK regulations, but please note that whether you live in the UK or not, your own particular area may have different controls. It's always essential to check what rules there are where you live. But the regulations described in this book will give you an idea of what to look out for.

TIP

CHECK YOUR PLANT NAMES!

Many trees and shrubs may have different variants or their names may vary in different countries. This is why using botanical names (often known as 'Latin plant names') is so helpful.

Botanical names do look daunting if you're not used to them, but you don't need to remember them. Just copy them and put the words into a search engine so you can check what you're buying. In this book, I'll recommend plants by both their botanical and common names, but when you are buying a plant, check its botanical name.

I'll also recommend plants that are common in the UK. If you live in other parts of the world, you will probably find the same plants but you need to use the botanical name as the common name may be different.

Botanical names are universal all over the world, so that people involved in the study or sale of plants can communicate accurately.

For example, there is a vigorous climber which is called 'Virginia creeper' in the UK, but referred to as 'Boston ivy' or 'Japanese creeper' elsewhere. Its botanical name is '*Parthenocissus tricuspidata*'.

And some people refer to a pretty white evergreen climber as Star Jasmine, while others call it Confederate Jasmine. But every plant grower knows it as *Trachelospermum jasminoides* – all over the world and in whatever language you are speaking.

So, to make sure you're really getting the plant you want, always check the botanical name on the label and look it up in a book or online.

CHAPTER 2
FENCES AND WALLS

There's a saying 'Good fences make good neighbours.'

This is because arguments over boundaries are a major source of tension between neighbours. The best way of reducing that tension is to have a clearly marked boundary with no doubt as to who owns what or who is responsible for upkeep. However, even if the boundary is your responsibility, it's always a good idea to let the neighbours know when you're doing work on it.

The first step to installing or replacing a hedge, fence or wall is to check whose responsibility it is to maintain that boundary. This should be in your Deeds or where the land is registered in your name, such as in the UK Land Registry.

If you don't have responsibility for maintaining that boundary, then you can build the boundary of your choice on your side of their fence or wall. If they have a fence and you want a hedge, then this is easy – you just plant the hedge on your side of the fence. If you want a fence or wall that is different from the one they want, then you can either ask them if you can pay to change the boundary, or you can build a second boundary on your side.

You also need to check the location of any pipes or cables before installing a new fence, unless you are just following the line of the old one exactly (and you're not digging fence posts any deeper!).

If you're worried about your neighbour's noise, then a hedge is often your best option, as planting muffles sound to some extent. Noise bounces against hard boundaries such as fences and walls, so they can make your own noise slightly worse for you. If you're on a busy road, then acoustic (noise-absorbent) fencing will usually reduce the noise level to some degree, especially if you add trees and shrubs on your side of the fence.

However, whether you live in the city, town or countryside, there will always be noise from outside your property and you will be able to hear it in your garden. The human ear usually adapts to a low or regular noise, and 'stops hearing it', which is why muffling a noise may be enough to stop you feeling upset by it, even if you can still actually hear it.

A solid fence or wall will maintain your privacy, but in many areas you may not be allowed to have one that is higher than around 2 metres (6ft 7"). This can reduce to 1 metre for a front garden. Check your local regulations. 2 metres normally gives you privacy at ground level, while 1 metre does not.

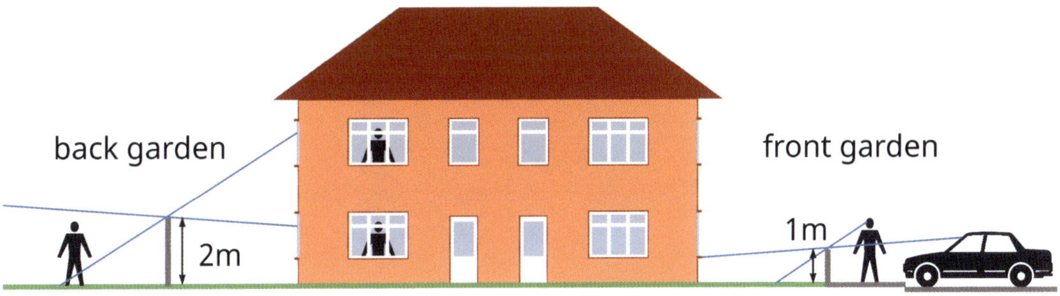

Standard Wall/Fence Heights

Many people add a trellis to the top of a fence or wall to increase privacy and to offer support to beautiful climbing plants. This is also a good security measure, because a trellis is not very strong or secure. It's likely to break if climbed on, and the broken bits of plants and trellis are harder to climb over than a clean fence or wall top. You may or may not need planning permission for a trellis in your area, so check. (See Chapter 5 on Screens for privacy).

You can paint or stain a fence to make it look more attractive. A black or dark blue fence is very contemporary and is a good backdrop for plants. A mid-blue fence can be charmingly rustic and a white fence will reflect light. However even if you are only painting the fence on your side, you need to check the legal situation. If you don't own the fence, you may need permission from your neighbour before you can paint it.

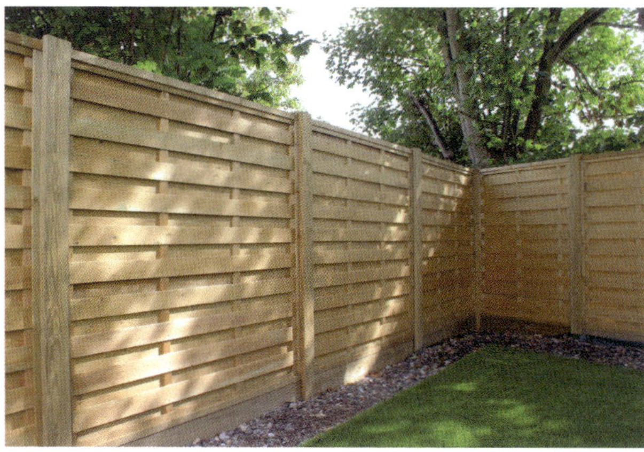

A Selection of Fence Patterns

Popular fence patterns include (*from top*): tongue and groove fencing, featherboard fencing and horizontal hit-and-miss. From Jackson's Fencing (jacksons-fencing.co.uk) Jacksons Fencing supply fencing, gates, decking, outdoor structures such as pergolas and trellis, plus security fencing and their Jakoustic noise barrier fencing.

YOUR NOTES

Attractive fences and suppliers

CHAPTER 3
HEDGES

There are many advantages to choosing a hedge rather than a fence, especially if you want to maximise privacy.

Hedges are effective at absorbing air pollution, they offer a habitat for wildlife and they help to soften the impact of neighbouring noise to some extent.

As gardens get smaller, there's always the temptation to save space by having a fence instead of a hedge. But hedges can be beautiful in themselves. The more plants you have in your garden, the better your air quality will be, and hedges offer sanctuary to wildlife – you'll be able to watch small birds darting in and out of your hedge, where they will be safe from predators. If you choose a mixed hedge, which has flowers and berries, then hedges also help pollinating insects and provide winter food for birds.

If you have a larger garden then hedges can sometimes also buffer wind better than a fence or a wall. This is because the wind is broken up when it blows through the hedge and its turbulence reduces beyond. If the wind hits a fence or a wall, there will be a wind-free area immediately on the other side of the wall, but it blows quickly over the wall, and it can be stronger some distance away from the wall. This is less likely to apply in a small garden, because the wind-free area immediately beside the wall or fence may be enough for wind protection. See chapter 10.

So hedges are pretty good!

All hedges will need clipping or pruning at least once a year, so they are a little more work than fences. However, fences often need re-painting or repairing. Everything needs some maintenance. Check our list of good hedging plants and avoid any that need clipping more than twice a year if you want to stay low-maintenance.

HERE IS THE LINK:
www.gov.im/media/416659/hedgeheightloss.pdf

HOW HIGH CAN YOUR HEDGE BE?

In many areas, hedges are subject to height restrictions. Generally, in the UK for example, an evergreen hedge should be no higher than 2 metres or 6ft 7". However, there is guidance from the Deputy Prime Minister's Office on how high a hedge should be before a council takes action to force the homeowner to reduce it.

This is a complex calculation, based on how big the garden is, how long the hedge is and how close the hedge is to the windows of the neighbours' house. It's been very carefully thought-out, with a view to balancing privacy and light, and considering both the homeowner and the neighbour.

It's worth consulting this document when you are trying to decide what is reasonable and fair.

However, it's only 'guidance', and a local council in the UK could still enforce a strict 2 metre restriction if it wanted to.

WHAT KIND OF HEDGE COULD YOU HAVE?

For many areas, the definition of a hedge is 'three trees in a row.' When considering a hedge, many people think of the classic formal hedge consisting of several similar plants which are clipped to a consistent design. But you can get a more natural look with an easier-to-maintain mixed informal hedge with different plants.

"Three Trees in a Row" – a definition of a hedge

Think about the shape of the shrub or tree. You'll save space at ground level and let in light for other plants if you choose a hedge which can be clipped so that its trunk is bare.

A 'pleached' hedge is very stylish. This is a row of trees, such as hornbeam or lime, which have bare trunks and their branches wired together and clipped. This looks a bit like a hedge on stilts!

And bamboo is a plant which is slender at the base with screening foliage at the top. Be careful only to choose bamboos that do not spread.

TYPES OF HEDGE

A formal, clipped hedge.

On the left of this garden there is an informal, natural hedge created by a number of different trees and plants. They are pruned but not clipped.

TYPES OF HEDGE

A pleached hedge. This is like a hedge on stilts, where the branches are trained to run together to create a smart geometric shape on top of bare trunks.

A winter hedge. Beech and hornbeam leaves of both die off in winter, but remain on the plant. Not 'evergreen' but they offer winter privacy.

TIP
BUY FROM THE EXPERTS!

I'd recommend buying hedges from a hedge or tree specialist rather than a general 'garden centre'. Look for a company whose experts are happy to advise you on what you want in your hedge, and who will make suggestions for hedging plants that should grow well in your climate and soil. They will also be able to tell you how to plant it, and may have a hedge planting service themselves.

DO YOU WANT YEAR-ROUND PRIVACY?

If you want year-round privacy from your hedge, then choose an evergreen or semi-evergreen hedge.

Here is a list of good plants for fast-growing evergreen hedges which grow well in most soils, unless otherwise stated. I'm giving the common name first, and then the botanical name. These long Latin or Greek based names may look unnecessary or daunting. However, before you make a final decision on a hedge, check the botanical name of the plant you're about to buy, and make sure it is the variety you want (see "TIP: Check your plant names!" in Chapter 1). Use the internet to match up the botanical name with the plant's characteristics. A hedge is a big investment in plants and common names can sometimes cover several different sorts of plant!

(Note: these are recommendations that are appropriate for temperate climates, such as the UK, Northern Europe, USA hardiness zones 8-10 and temperate parts of Southern Australia and New Zealand).

Leylandii cypress (*Cupressuscyparis leylandii*).

A very fast-growing evergreen conifer - widely disliked, but it can be a good hedge if trimmed at least once a year. Can be cut into formal clipped shapes. But they can grow up to 100ft, creating deep shade. In the UK, Leylandii hedge are legally limited to 2m high (although see above "How high can your hedge be?"). Tolerates wind and cold. Good for absorbing pollution. Several different leaf colour variants.

Laurel - Cherry laurel, English laurel, common laurel (*Prunus laurocerasus* x variants).

Laurel is also very fast-growing and will grow in most conditions and soil types (except very alkaline soil). Tolerates wind, cold and shade. It can be clipped into shape or left as an informal hedge. Will grow to 18ft if left untrimmed. Also check out Portuguese laurel (*Prunus lusitanica*).

Firethorn (*Pyracantha*).

A fast-growing prickly hedge with wonderful red, yellow or orange berries in autumn. Grows up to 10ft if not trimmed. Often recommended as a 'security hedge'.

Griselinia littoralis (no common name)

A bright 'apple green' hedge which does well in coastal climates and tolerates most conditions. Medium-fast growing. Can be trimmed into a formal shape. Grows up to 18ft if not trimmed.

Red Robin (*Photinia x fraseri* 'Red Robin')

A fast-growing evergreen with distinctive red leaves. Grows up to 15ft if not trimmed.

Western Red Cedar (*Thuja plicata*)

Another very fast-growing conifer that can get to 100ft, but can regenerate from old wood (so if it's out of control, you have a better chance of cutting it back and re-shaping it). Several leaf colour variants.

SEMI-EVERGREEN HEDGING AND OTHER GOOD HEDGING OPTIONS

Privet (*Ligustrum ovalifolium*)

Is a classic hedging choice. It can be clipped into shapes, but it does lose some or all its leaves in a harsh winter, so can only be considered semi-evergreen. Will grow almost anywhere, including exposed places, although it doesn't like very damp sites. Fast-growing so will need clipping twice a year.

Hornbeam (*Carpinus betulus*)

Its leaves change colour in winter, but it holds onto them so it is considered semi-evergreen and will provide a privacy screen even in winter. An excellent hedge for exposed sites, damp soils, shady places and other difficult locations. Good for wildlife if left unclipped.

Beech (*Fagus sylvatica*)

Another good hedge which holds most of its leaves throughout winter. Bright green leaves in the spring and beautiful copper/brown foliage in winter. There are also purple and copper beech variants.

Evergreen wildlife hedges

The Wildlife Trusts say that using hedging rather than fences offers food and shelter for wildlife. Keep hedges informal to allow flowers and berries to develop. Many good wildlife friendly hedging plants are deciduous (hawthorn, blackthorn, dog rose, field maples). However holly, ivy, Viburnum tinus and evergreen honeysuckle will give you year-round interest and privacy. Use a range of different plants and leave mainly unclipped for a good wildlife hedge.

Another good hedge is Box (*Buxus sempervirens*) but it is currently affected by the spread of box tree caterpillar and box blight. Yew is also popular, but is slower growing than the other plants listed here. Holly can also be grown as a prickly 'security hedge', but it is slow growing.

Tall plants and summer flowers almost completely shield this seating area in the garden at Gravetye Manor Hotel in Sussex. Tall planting like this can also provide summer privacy to ground floor windows.

PRIVACY IN THE SUMMER ONLY?

Deciduous hedging is hedging that loses all its leaves every winter. If you want year round privacy, you probably don't want deciduous hedging. If you do, there are huge number of options. Many trees and shrubs can be planted in a row to create a hedge.

In the United Kingdom, restrictions usually apply only to evergreen hedges, so if you're happy to have a deciduous hedge, which loses its leaves in the winter, then your hedge can be higher. Some hedging plants, such as hornbeam and beech, count as deciduous because their leaves die in winter, although they hold onto them. So you can get year-round coverage.

Bamboo and ivy are also not covered by the UK's High Hedges Act. However, don't just choose the option that will give you the highest hedge or fence. Your garden will be darker and you may upset your neighbours. Start your privacy with your hedge, fence or wall, but look at other options beyond that.

HERE ARE THE FACTORS TO THINK ABOUT WHEN CHOOSING A HEDGE

- Will your hedge grow in sun or shade? If shade, make sure your hedging plant is suitable.
- Do you want spring flowers and/or autumn colour? Check the label or ask the grower.
- Do you want a fast-growing hedge? If so, remember that it will need more maintenance with regular clipping, once it is fully grown. Check the ultimate height.
- A mixed wildlife hedge? Combine plants with flowers and berries together. Keep them loosely pruned so you don't cut off too many flowers or berries. Hawthorn, blackthorn, wild roses, wild cherries or cherry plum, hazel, crab apple, beech, spindle and buckthorn are all recommended for wildlife in the UK.

SHADY SPOT?

Is your hedge going to be in a shady spot? If so, it's important to choose hedging plants that are happy in shade. People often forget what conditions their hedges need.

If you have a shady garden, plants that should do well include: hornbeam, holly, yew, laurel (cherry laurel and Portuguese laurel) and Viburnum tinus.

Many of the other hedging plants listed here do well in partial shade, but check with the grower to make sure that your particular situation is suitable for them.

DAMP SOIL?

And is it damp where you plan to plant the hedge? That's important, as very few hedging plants will be happy in very damp conditions. Willow is probably the best choice for very damp soil, but it's not evergreen. if your soil is only slightly damp, then you may be able to grow one of the Laurel family or Western Red Cedar as a hedge.

These two crab apple trees (*Malus hupehensis*) in the front garden give front window privacy, blossom in the spring and crab apple fruits in autumn.

GROWTH SPEED

The next questions to ask are 'how fast will my hedge grow?' and 'how high will it get?' And you need to ask whether it is evergreen (keeps its leaves all year round) or deciduous (loses its leaves in winter). If you live in a very windy place, near the coast (with salt air) or on a polluted main road, check that the hedging plant is happy in those conditions.

If you want a hedge to fill the space quickly, then you either need a fast-growing hedge or you can buy an 'instant hedge'. But be aware that a fast-growing hedge will need clipping at least twice a year or it may get too big.

An 'instant' hedge is a line of mature hedge bushes, delivered to your house. These should preferably be installed by a hedge supplier. This kind of hedge will need extra care, such as more watering, in its first year or two, especially if you live in a dry area. Larger plants need more water than small, young ones, and they won't have enough root area to support their needs.

So you'll have to water until their roots grow. An instant hedge will cost about ten times as much as planting young hedging plants.

If you buy a 'fast-growing' hedge, you can expect it to grow 40-60cm a year. That's approximately one to two feet a year.

CLIMBING HEDGE PLANTS

You can also create a hedge with climbing plants over a trellis or frame. Ivy and Star Jasmine are two good 'climbing' hedge choices. See our list of good climbing plants for screens and hedges in Chapter 7.

BAMBOO

Bamboo is fast growing, elegant and occupies relatively little space at ground level. However, it can be very invasive and it's essential to check for that in the variety you are buying. You don't want bamboo invading your entire garden.

You should also have bamboos planted by a specialist, with a non-perishable root control barrier dug into the earth. But I have heard of gardens where even that doesn't work! You could also have bamboos in large pots, and that can work very well. They won't escape, but they will also be less dense.

Bamboo species vary, and you should choose ones that are described as non-invasive. However, it's often a good idea to have a root

barrier installed even with the least invasive bamboo species. Bamboos prefer not to compete with other garden plants so a row of bamboos planted as a screen is a good way to grow them. Bamboos are evergreen, but can often look very scrappy in winter.

The least invasive bamboos include Black bamboo (*Phyllostachys nigra*) and Umbrella bamboo (*Fargesia scabrida* 'Asian Wonder').

A MIXED HEDGE

If you want your garden to be wildlife-friendly, then a mixed hedge is best as it helps bio-diversity. For a reasonably fast-growing evergreen mixed hedge, combine plants such as holly, privet, beech, pyracantha, photinia and laurel. Some companies sell mixed packs of hedges.

PRICKLY 'SECURITY' HEDGE

While a determined burglar won't be put off by a hedge, a row of prickly bushes will certainly discourage the casual trouble-maker. Prickly evergreen hedges include pyracantha, berberis and holly. However, note that berberis and holly are medium growers and will probably only grow around a foot a year (40cm). If you want to add non-evergreens to your spiky hedge, then consider dog roses, hawthorn and blackthorn.

PLANTING YOUR HEDGE

A hedge is easy to plant and look after, but you will need to keep it watered regularly in its first summer until it grows its roots properly into the soil. When planting it, add plenty of compost and follow the growers' instructions. How your hedge grows depends on your soil and whether it has the right amount of sun and shade, so that's why it's worth asking the grower when you're choosing a hedge. Hedges on very heavy clay soils may need different planting techniques from those on light, sandy soils, for example.

If you are digging trenches or deep holes for your hedge, check for underground cabling and pipes before you dig. Hedge roots are unlikely to damage cables and drains as they grow, unless there is already a problem. But it's important not to damage pipework or cables when you're digging.

YOUR NOTES

Your hedges shortlist – what you really like.

CHAPTER 4
TREES

Trees are a great option for creating more privacy. But some people worry that they will block the light or cause damage to buildings.

The Royal Horticultural Society (the RHS) says that incidences of trees damaging buildings are very rare. But it makes sense not to plant a tree very close to a garden wall or a house wall. In theory, a tree should be planted three quarters of its final height away from a building.See the following diagrams, including how to assess the height of an existing tree.

It's very unlikely that tree roots will damage drains, cables or pipes. However, when you are digging the hole to plant the tree, make sure that you don't accidentally cause any damage to your services yourself.

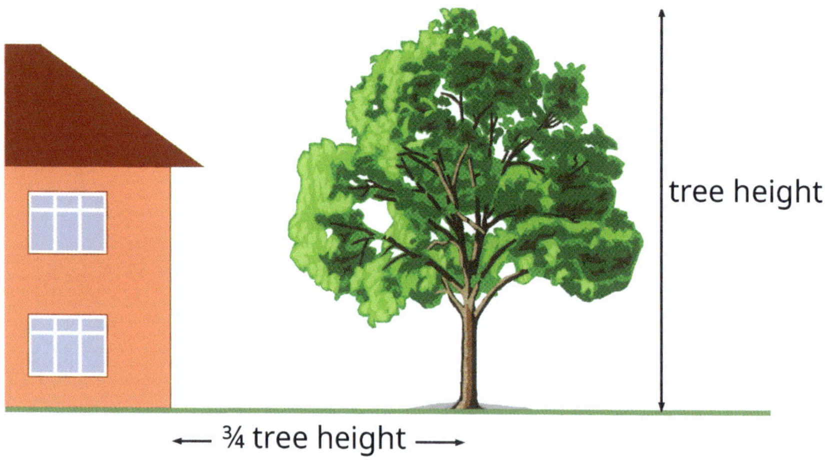

Tree Proximity Rule

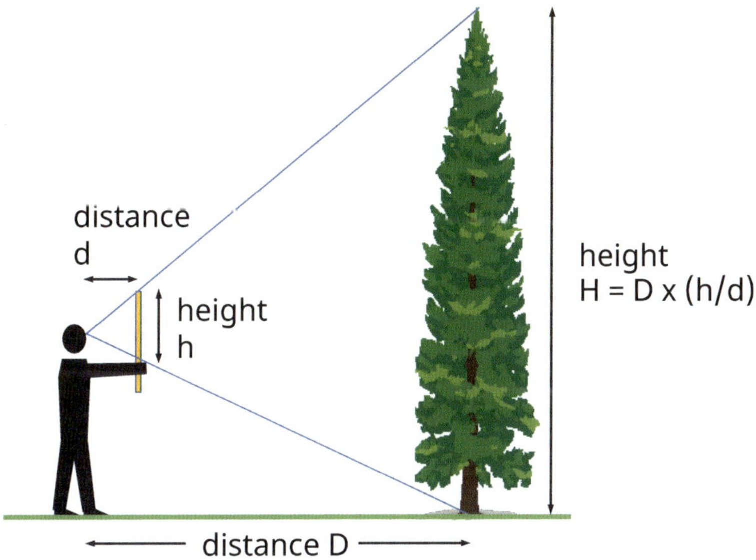

Measuring Tree Height

CHOOSE THE RIGHT SHAPED TREE

Trees grow naturally into different shapes. If you are short of space, then choose a tree which doesn't have much growth around the base. You may also be able to cut off the lower branches (known as 'lifting the tree's crown') to create more light at ground level.

Look at the sightline and how the shape of the tree can give you more privacy. A single narrow tree, such as a fastigiate or columnar tree may be all you need if you are interrupting the sight line from a single window. But a vase shaped or umbrella shaped tree may be best to create privacy for your own upper windows.

Assess how much sun or shade your tree will have and choose a tree that is happy with that. And consider what you might wish to plant around the base. You'll generally get more light on the ground with a vase shape or an umbrella shape. Always check the final height of the tree and how long it takes to grow to that height. Many trees can be trimmed into the required shape – for example, magnolia grandiflora is naturally a pyramidal shape but can be turned into a 'lollipop' or spreading shape by removing the lower branches.

TREE SHAPES

Horizontal Spreading

Fastigiate

Open-Head Irregular

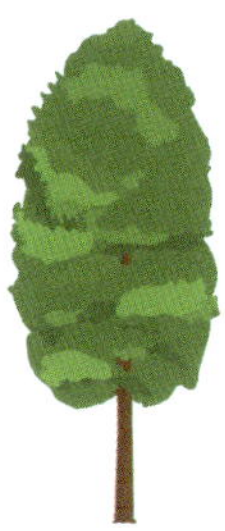

Columnar

Umbrella

Globe/Round

Weeping

Pyramidal

Vase

Two trees flank a contemporary arched bench-arbour in this garden designed by Dave Green. The trees are planted away from the boundaries and turn this small space into a secret garden.

WHERE TO POSITION A TREE FOR PRIVACY

Trees for privacy do not have to be planted on your boundary. The boundary may not even be the best place for them, as they may not be effective there. And neighbours may not want a tree so close to their land.

The most important thing is to decide where you want to be private. Then plant the tree as close to that space as possible, rather than close to the over-looking window or boundary. The further away a tree is, the higher it will have to be before it makes that part of your garden more private. Even a single 5ft high screen can make an eating area quite private if it's close to the table and chairs.

You can also place a tree in the middle of a lawn or flower border, as part of your design. As it grows, it will cast some shade, but there are many shade-loving plants. And a shady bed is easier to look after – plants, including weeds, grow more slowly.

But the first thing to establish is where you want to be private – your primary and secondary privacy spaces – and who is going to overlook you when you are there. Is there a row of windows or just one single window?

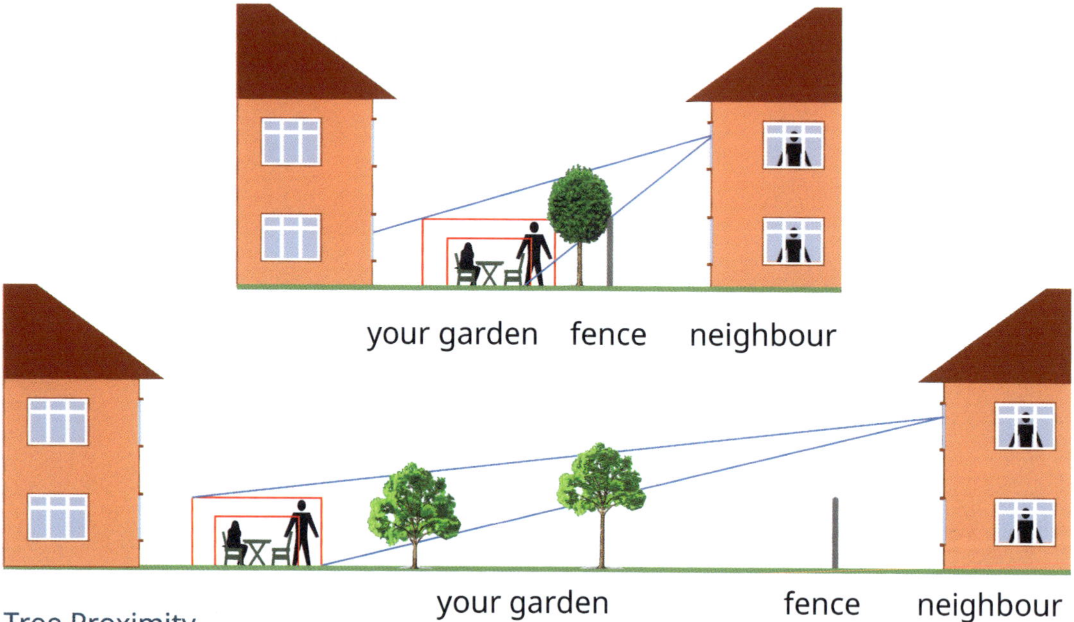

Tree Proximity

Now use our diagram to see how high your tree needs to be and where it could be placed.

If it seems odd to place a tree in that position, it may be worth getting a garden designer in to plan your garden. It's also helpful to look at garden designs, blog posts, Pinterest and magazine articles to give you ideas on how a tree might look placed in a particular spot.

WHEN DO YOU WANT YOUR GARDEN PRIVACY?

Many people use deciduous trees to screen the windows of their homes. The leaves fall off in winter, but in the Northern hemisphere, days are short. You close your curtains and turn on the light early in the evening and open the curtains relatively late in the morning. So you may not need privacy in the winter during daylight hours. And in winter, the

This garden by Caitlin McLoughlin uses a combination of hedging, abundant summer planting and a small deciduous tree to create a secluded space.

extra light is welcome, while on a hot summer day you may be happy to be shaded.

Trees in leaf help to cool nearby buildings during hot weather. Evergreen trees help to insulate buildings from cold and wind in winter. So your choice of tree may also impact on the temperature inside your house and even help your heating or air conditioning bills!

The same goes for garden privacy. If you only sit out in your garden in summer, then perhaps it doesn't matter that there are no leaves in winter. That would give you a wider range of trees to choose from. It also means you can choose trees with beautiful blossom, such as fruit trees or deciduous magnolias.

Always check the label before buying to find out how high the tree will grow and whether it is fast or slow-growing.

Plant labels sometimes don't have much information on them, or the information may not be entirely accurate. Once you have a shortlist of trees or plants you like, find out their botanical names and look them up on the internet to make sure you're buying the size and type of tree or plant you really want. See "TIP: Check your plant names!" in Chapter 1.

I've given the botanical names after the common names here.

FIVE OF THE BEST EVERGREEN TREES FOR PRIVACY

Southern magnolia (*Magnolia grandiflora*).

Its large, thick, glossy leaves and pyramidal shape create a solid barrier to light. Slow to medium growing and can reach up to 90ft/27m high.

Red Robin (*Photinia x fraseri* 'Red Robin').

Red tinged leaves and pretty white flowers make this an ornamental choice. Many people grow this as a shrub or a hedge, but it can be allowed to grow into a small tree. Can be cut into shapes.

Holm Oak (*Quercus Ilex*).
Easy to grow and moderately fast growing, these can get to 40ft/12m if left untrimmed. They are globe/rounded shaped. Respond well to regular pruning. You can even clip them into topiary shapes or lollipop-type domes.

Cherry laurel (*Prunus laurocerasus*).
Easy to grow, fast-growing standard shaped tree with glossy green leaves. Can grow up to 25ft/8m if left untrimmed.

Fortune's Osmanthus (*Osmanthus x fortunei*).
Good small tree for privacy with an oval shape and dark green leaves. Prefers a sheltered spot. Slow growing, but can grow up to 25ft/8m. Scented jasmine-like flowers.

FIVE OF THE BEST DECIDUOUS TREES FOR PRIVACY

Ornamental pear (*Pyrus calleyrana 'Chanticleer'*) –
A vase shaped tree that grows even in coastal or windy areas and deals with pollution well. It's considered the 'perfect street tree' because it never gets too big or spreading.

Ornamental plum (*Prunus cerasifera*).
There are several good ornamental plum trees, such as the Black Cherry Plum, a very pretty tree with dark red leaves, beautiful spring blossom and good autumn colour. Vase-shaped when young but gets more rounded and spreading with age.

Norway maple (*Acer platanoides 'Globosum'*) –
A small tree with a dense, round crown. Its mid-green leaves turn a strong late-season yellow. Many maples (Acers) are slow-growing, so they're useful if you want a tree that will stay compact. But don't choose a maple for a fast-growing privacy tree unless you're going to buy it the size you want it to be.

Crab apples, especially Malus 'Gorgeous' or 'Red Sentinel',
which hold onto their fruit during the winter and

Malus 'Hupehensis'
which needs very little pruning to keep it in an attractive vase shape.

Apple or pear trees grown as espaliers.

SHOULD I BUY A YOUNG TREE OR ONE THAT IS ALREADY THE HEIGHT I NEED?

There are two very big advantages to buying small, young trees. Firstly they are much cheaper and secondly they grow better and are less likely to be blown over.

The roots of a tall, mature tree have to support more weight and height. So it won't be fully secure until those roots have grown properly down into the soil. It will need to be very well supported for the first few years. It will also need extra watering, and it won't grow much until its roots are sorted out. It will be much more expensive.

However, if a mature tree is planted and supported properly, you will get an instant tree height and exactly the effect you want immediately. If you buy a full size, mature tree, it is worth getting it planted professionally. It will be expensive, but your tree is much more likely to survive and do well if it is professionally planted.

DO YOU ALREADY HAVE THE RIGHT TREE?

If you already have trees in your garden, but you don't like them, think about whether you can have them shaped or trimmed. It is much easier and quicker – and probably cheaper – to work on a tree that is already growing in your garden than buying a new one.

Get a tree shaped and trimmed by a qualified tree surgeon or arborist (sometimes referred to as an arboriculturalist). There are arboricultural associations in most countries, with a list of qualified members. If you get your tree pruned by someone who is only qualified to use a chain saw rather than qualified in proper tree surgery, the result can be ugly and could damage the tree's shape.

When talking to tree experts, see if they are listening to what you want. If you don't understand something, ask them to explain it again. We are all experts in different things, so we all need a bit of extra explanation sometimes. And beware the man with a chain saw who just wants to cut everything down!

YOUR NOTES

Note down your favourite tree recommendations or shapes.

CHAPTER 5
SCREENS

If you have decided on your boundary, and planted one or more trees in your garden, you may still feel that your garden isn't quite private enough.

Take a look at our explanation of Primary and Secondary Privacy space in Chapter 1 to remind yourself about how to make certain areas of your garden very private, while accepting that complete privacy may not be possible in other areas.

This is where screens come in. Today's manmade screens can be very attractive. You can also create living screens made of plants, for example planting up a trellis or pergola, espaliered fruit trees or low hedging. You can even screen an area with tall plants.

ADD TRELLIS TO YOUR WALL OR FENCE

You can often add a layer of privacy to your wall or fence by adding trellis on top. In some areas, you don't need planning permission to do this, but elsewhere you may need planning permission if you want to increase the height of your wall or fence by adding trellis.

There are lots of different sorts of trellis. You can get basic trellis quite inexpensively at garden centres, but don't forget that a trellis is only as strong as the posts it is set onto.

Square, diamond and slatted trellis

You can buy square lattice or diamond-patterned trellis, or a trellis made of horizontal slats with gaps in between. The more substantial the wood feels, the longer the trellis will last.

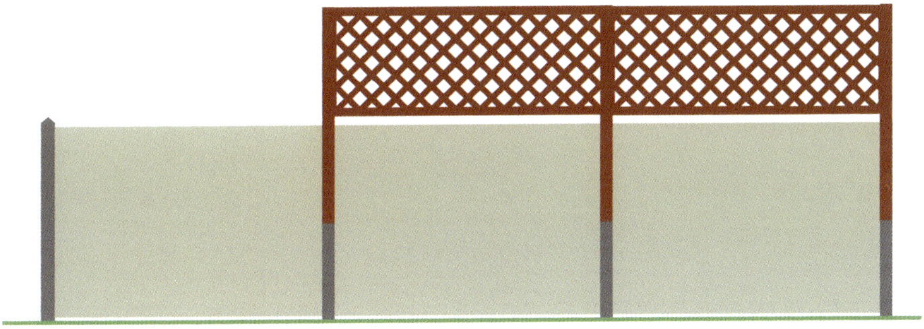

A Trellis for Raising the Privacy from a Fence

You can also use trellis – properly supported – to create screening around a pergola or as a stand-a-lone feature. However, make sure that it is properly secured. If you just add some trellis above a planting box, the wind will probably blow it over once it’s covered in plants.

WHAT YOU NEED TO KNOW ABOUT INSTALLING TRELLIS

There are lots of tutorials for installing DIY trellis on the internet. If you check several, you should get a good idea of which one to go for. Or use a qualified professional company to install the trellis. They should do it properly, but it's good to have a broad idea of what ought to be happening.

Posts for supporting trellis should usually be dug around 2ft into the ground. They are fixed into the ground with a special fast-drying concrete mix designed specifically for posts (often called Post Mix). You can get it at builder's merchants.

You can also support trellis on top of a wall with posts secured to fixings on the wall, but only if the wall is strong and in good condition. The trellis itself shouldn't be too high – no higher than 0.9m or 3ft. And the fixing posts need to be one size bigger than the trellis – for example a 0.9m high panel of trellis needs at least 1.2m (4ft) of post to secure it to the wall.

Trellis must be kept vertical – it puts a strain on it to have it sloping. Tip: When planting up a trellis, check how big your climber grows – some very vigorous climbers can grow 40ft or more. And they can get very bulky if you don't prune them back. If you let very vigorous climbers get out of control, you can create a 'sail' effect where the vegetation is so bulky that it catches the wind and pulls the trellis down.

A homemade screen of corrugated iron and timber boards hides a washing line.

Rustic arches in a house in Spain offer some privacy without blocking all the light. An example of a 'broken screen' which is surprisingly effective, especially when covered with plants.

HOW TO CHOOSE A CLIMBER FOR TRELLIS OR SCREEN

If you are choosing climbers for screening, look at the way they grow. For example, wisteria shoots up and all the action is at the top where the flowers are. You wouldn't get a lot of screening lower down from wisteria. Look for climbers that spread sideways as well as up (such as ivy) if you're looking for screening, or climbers that can be trained sideways, such as roses.

Always remember to check whether the position you're planting the climber in is sunny or shady and choose the plant appropriately. It takes climbers a couple of years to grow. So you don't want to wait a few years for your climber to screen your trellis, only to realise that it is never going to grow happily.

Many climbers are deciduous and will lose their leaves in winter. If you're happy only to have summer screening, then you have a great deal of choice for climbers – climbing roses that can be trained to go sideways as well as up, for example. Espalier pruned fruit trees, too, make excellent deciduous climbers for screening. In winter their bare branches look spare but in summer the leaves and fruit completely cover the area.

GOOD EVERGREEN CLIMBERS FOR TRELLIS:

Star jasmine/Confederate jasmine (*Trachelospermum jasminoides*).

This has dark green foliage and sweetly scented white flowers. It can be trained along a trellis to give full cover. Prefers sun but can cope with part shade. The foliage turns bronze in autumn.

Armand clematis (*Clematis armandii*).

A vigorous evergreen clematis with white flowers. Needs a sheltered spot and should be grown in full sun, but it's hardy down to Zone 4.

Evergreen honeysuckle (*Lonicera nitida*).

A fast-growing evergreen honeysuckle with small white flowers. Makes an excellent hedge or screen. Will grow in sun and shade. It can be clipped into neat shapes and is often called 'Poor Man's Yew' because it can be made into topiary.

Ivy (*Hedera* +).

Ivy is a vigorous climber which will spread easily. It grows in most soils, in sun and in shade, and it's very wildlife friendly. But it can work its roots into cracks in poor masonry or around guttering, so people avoid it for buildings. As a cover for a trellis, there are fewer concerns although the weight of it might bring some trellis down in a strong wind if it's not maintained properly. It would work very well to cover any form of chicken wire or other wire screen. Ivy has different variants of leaf shade and pattern. The Royal Horticultural Society are doing trials on using ivy as a cover for buildings when grown on a protective copper mesh or zinc screen. The screen stops the ivy from penetrating any masonry or causing damage.

Climbing Hydrangeas.

Hydrangeas can be evergreen or deciduous. However evergreen climbing hydrangeas are unusual. There is one called *Hydrangea seemannii*, and there is also a relative of the hydrangea *Decumaria sinensis*. Hydrangeas will grow in sun or shade and can be hardy down to Zone 4, although their hardiness varies according to type, so you'll need to check. This is why using the botanical names is important! (see Chapter 1).

Fretwork wood composite screens, such as those made by Screen With Envy (screenwithenvy.co.uk) create private corners, such as this one designed by Pip Probert.

OTHER TYPES OF MANMADE SCREENS

A five foot high screen near your primary privacy space can make a big difference. If it's in front of a table, or to the side, you probably won't be seen while you're all sitting down. But it needn't block out all the light.

You can get laser-cut metal screens, plain metal screens, slatted screens, wood and willow screens, living screens and more. You could build a short section of wall out of bricks, concrete or stone. Or you could create a living screen with trellis or chicken wire and plant it up.

Laser-cut metal screens are decorative and add to privacy, such as this one by Stark & Greensmith (starkandgreensmith.com), seen at the RHS Hampton Court Garden Festival.

LIVING SCREENS

You'll sometimes see the phrase 'living screens' used. It just means a screen covered with plants, so everything that applies to trellis and to hedging also applies to living screens. Usually a wire mesh screen is covered with climbing or hedging plants. Good plants for a living screen include the good evergreen hedging plants in Chapter 3 and evergreen climbers in this chapter. You will need to trim a living screen at least once a year.

A SUMMER HEDGE

Another kind of 'living screen' is sometimes called a summer hedge. This is when some plants in a border are so tall that they screen a bench or table. Tall grasses, such as miscanthus, can make a summer hedge, or a row of larger cannas.

But if you want to use border plants for screening, remember that flowers usually only last a few weeks. Tall flowers, such as foxgloves and delphiniums, will only give you screening for a few weeks a year. So look at the foliage and the structure of the plant to find one that will screen you for at least the summer months.

WHAT IS AN ESPALIERED TREE?

An espaliered tree is grown on a framework. Branches are trained to go right and left, but any branches sticking out on either side are cut off. So the tree is almost two dimensional. It's an excellent way to grow fruit because all the fruit gets lots of sunlight and ripens well. And you get a living fence of apple or pear branches.

YOUR NOTES

Blank space where you can write the names of companies making privacy screens that you like. Also you can draw diagrams showing where the screens could go in your garden.

CHAPTER 6
OTHER STRUCTURES

Garden structures, such as sheds, arches, pergolas, gazebos, arbours, sails and parasols can help make your garden more private. And if you want to make one part of your garden completely private (your primary privacy space, see chapter 1), they're often essential.

SHEDS AND OTHER GARDEN BUILDINGS

Once again, many places have regulations about how high garden structures can be. In the UK, your shed, greenhouse or other garden building cannot be higher than 2.5 metres (8ft 2") if it is within 2 metres of your boundary. If it is further than 2 metres from your boundary wall, it can be up to 4 metres (13ft) high.

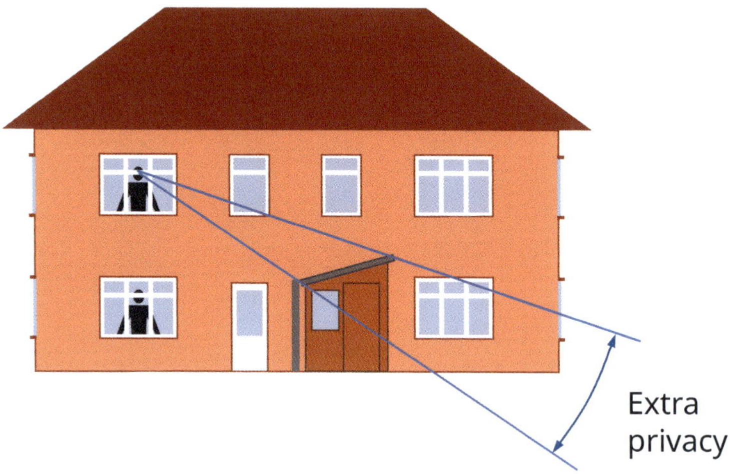

A Shed for Side Privacy

But if you live in a Listed Building, a conservation area or an Area of Outstanding Natural Beauty, you may have different rules or may have to apply for planning permission. Check with your local authority.

And, of course, wherever you live in the world, there may be specific rules you need to know about, often dating from when your house was built or your district was laid out. Check them before ordering a new garden building.

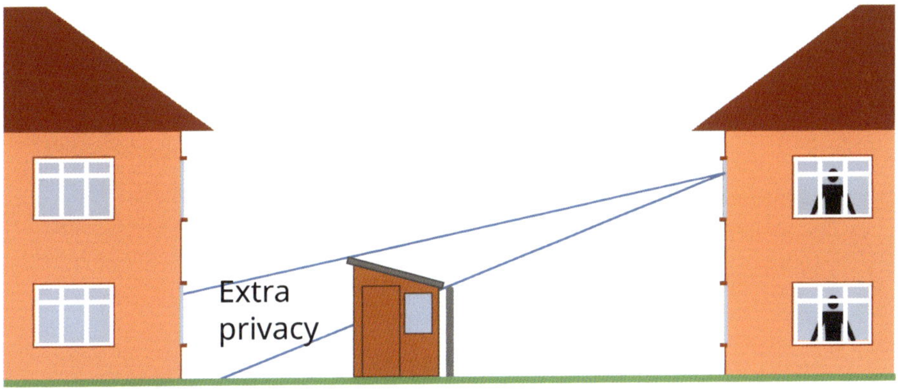

A Shed for Back Privacy

A garden building, such as a shed or greenhouse, needs a good secure base. You can buy sheds online or from garden centres but consider the base separately. If a wooden shed sits on the ground, it will ultimately rot as the damp from the ground will penetrate the wood.

A wooden base will delay this but will ultimately rot itself. A brick or concrete base prevents this.
It's also important to make sure the base is level. If it is slightly sloping or it sinks, then the shed's structure will be put under extra pressure over the years.

Think about where to place your shed to maximise your privacy. Your first thought may be to tuck the shed out of sight or at the bottom of the garden. But a shed can be very attractive. Make a feature of it by using it to block a sightline or cover up an eyesore.

Paint your garden shed, add bunting or salvaged architectural features. Grow climbers up it on a trellis. Make a 'plant theatre' by adding shelves to the outside and displaying plants on it.

You can also use the shed to divide the garden. If you want to create a 'secret garden' space, then use the shed as part of what divides the space from the rest of the garden. For example a narrow garden with a shed three quarters of the way down it will create a 'secret garden' space behind. In the past, these would have been used to disguise a working area. But you could add an arch, some trellis or a doorway. Then furnish with a comfortable lounger, table and chairs or a swinging bench, and fill with pollinator-friendly plants. You have created your own private haven.

Simple but effective metal arches at the Peter Beales Rose Garden in Norfolk, UK.

ARCHES

An arch must be high enough for a tall person to walk through them, even once there is planting twined round it. In theory, it should also be wide enough for two people to walk through it together, although lots of arches aren't this wide.

Choose between metal arches and pressure-treated timber. Pressure-treated timber lasts longer than ordinary wood. Metal arches may not be as strong as sturdy wooden ones.

PERGOLAS

A pergola is an open structure which supports climbing plants. A very simple pergola would have four legs, held together by crossbeams at roof height. You can add trellis to the side of a pergola.

A pergola can also be a walkway created by a series of arches. This can look beautiful when trained with climbing plants. Add seating underneath, creating the perfect private space for reading or meditating.

If your area has regulations about the heights of walls and fences, it will usually also have regulations about other garden structures. Pergolas and arches can usually be higher than walls and fences, although do check what the rules are in your area.

A pergola walkway down the side of your garden or a pergola at the end could increase your privacy, especially in primary privacy areas. And when you are sitting under a pergola, the climbing plants will generally help keep you private.

A Pergola Showing Maximum Height Next to a Boundary

ARBOURS

A garden arbour is somewhere between an arch and a pergola. It's usually something to walk through, though it sometimes has a bench with perhaps a trellis to the sides and overhead.

An arbour creates a little private spot in even the most crowded gardens. You can have a single fixed bench, a bench that curves or is L-shaped, or even a swing bench. Depending on the regulations where you live, they can be higher than fences or trellis.

Make sure that the arbour is installed on a flat piece of land and that it's fully secured, or the wind will blow it over. Good quality arbours will come with installation instructions or you can ask a professional.

When deciding where to place an arbour, remember that you will need to be able to reach it to paint or repair it every few years. Also consider the prevailing winds and make sure you make it as sheltered as possible. See Chapter 10 for advice on protecting your garden from wind.

GAZEBOS

A gazebo is a wooden garden shelter with a roof. It may or may not have one, two or three sides, but at least one side will be open to the garden. (If it had four sides and a door, it would be called a shed or garden room!)

Some definitions of Gazebo and Pergola say that a gazebo is round or octagonal while a pergola is square or rectangular. Many gazebos are round or octagonal, but it's the presence of a solid roof that makes it a gazebo rather than a pergola.

A gazebo gives you a weatherproof place where you can enjoy your garden. It can be an attractive design. And, in the UK, the gazebo roof can be higher than a fence or wall. A flat roofed gazebo can be 3 metres high, provided that it is at least 2m from your boundary. Or if it has a sloping roof, the highest part of the slope can be 4 metres high. If you live in an area with specific regulations, such as a Conservation area or a Listed Building, then you may need planning permission for a gazebo.

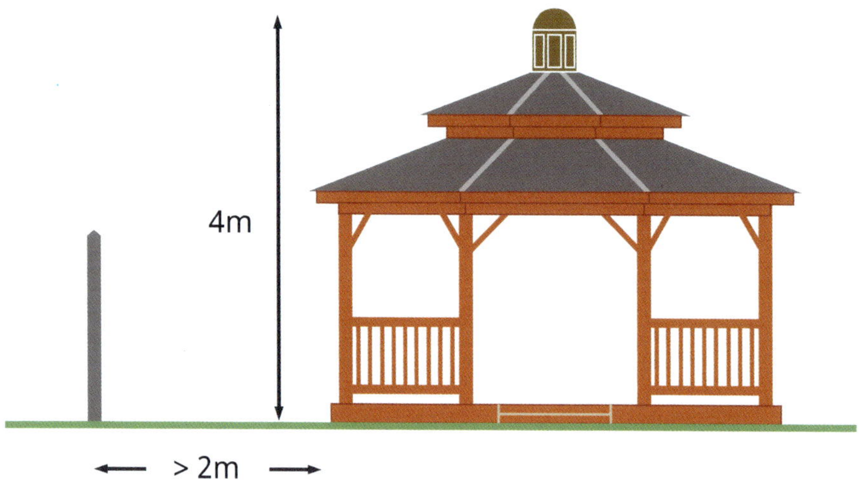

A Gazebo Showing Maximum Height Near a Boundary

A contemporary gazebo in the Viking Cruises Lagom show garden at RHS Hampton Court Garden Festival. The flat roof is a 'green roof.'

When you are under a gazebo roof, even if it has open sides, then you will be much more private. It's unlikely that people will even be able to see you, even from high windows. It interrupts the sight line. A gazebo can be a wonderful option if you want a space to exercise, meditate or do yoga, because you can give it a floor (lawn turf can be somewhat uneven).

One way of adding height to your 'boundary' and increase your privacy is to have a 2m wide path with planting next to the fence or wall. Then have a gazebo with a 4m high roof slope rising into your garden.

POP-UP GAZEBOS

Pop-up gazebos cost around the same as a good garden parasol. They offer much more privacy and protection from the elements. You are not supposed to leave a pop-up gazebo up overnight or for weeks at a time. You may invalidate the product guarantee if you do.

But people do leave pop-up gazebos up. I don't recommend it, but it could be a way of deciding whether you want a permanent structure. If you plan to use your pop-up gazebo frequently, look for one with extra reinforced fabric where you pull the canopy over the frame. Check that the material is waterproof, not just water resistant. And you will probably find it helpful if it has adjustable legs.

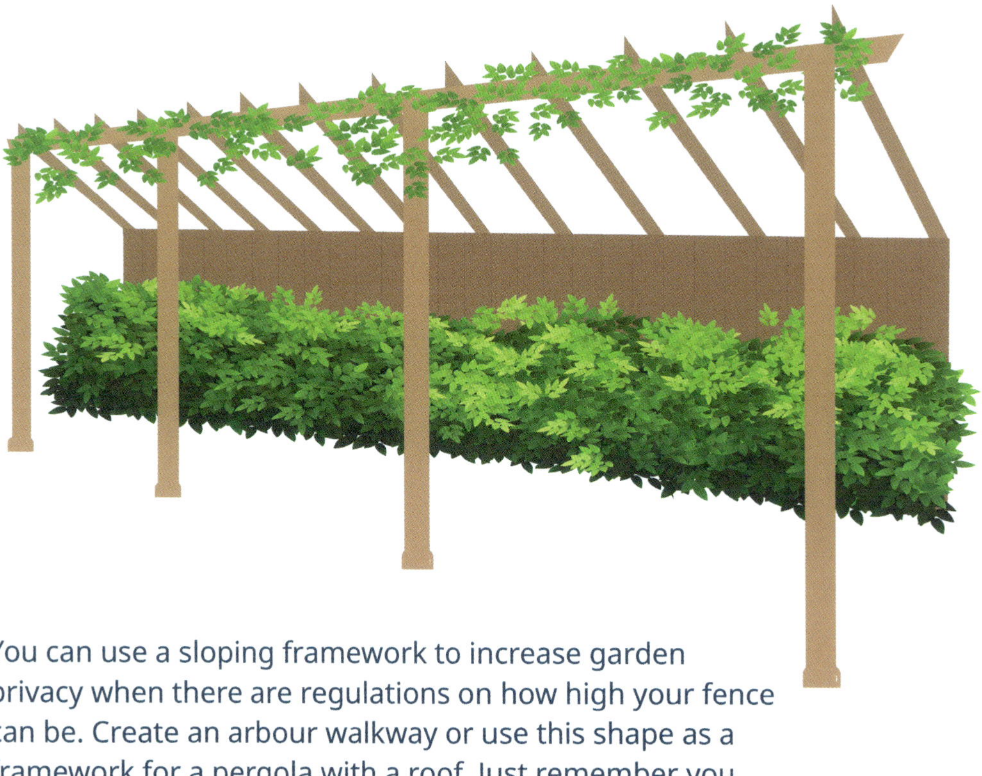

You can use a sloping framework to increase garden privacy when there are regulations on how high your fence can be. Create an arbour walkway or use this shape as a framework for a pergola with a roof. Just remember you need to comply with regulations on how high a structure can be and how far the roofline is from your boundary.

Garden Parasol

Banana Parasol

PRIVACY FROM PARASOLS AND SAIL SHADES

All forms of sunshade also increase your privacy. If you have a parasol beside or in the centre of your table, then anyone looking at your garden from windows above will not be able to see through it.

When choosing a parasol, it's just a question of matching your budget to your taste. You can choose from traditional 'umbrella' style parasols which are central to a heavy base. They often come up through a hole in the middle of your table. Or there are new 'banana' shaped cantilevered parasols. These are adjustable and hang over your table or lounger from the side. Both types of parasols come in budget and luxury options. If you're able to pay more, check how easy the parasol is to adjust and how hard-wearing it seems.

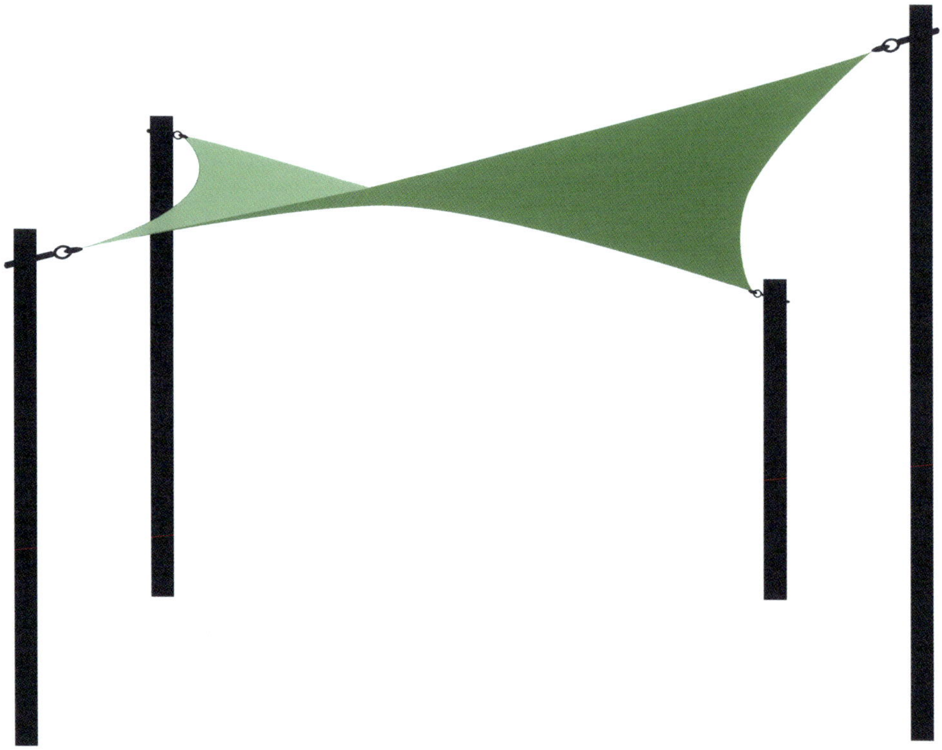

Sail Shade

SAIL SHADES

A sail shade is a little more complicated as it is a square or triangular piece of fabric that attaches to your house. Unless you already have secure fixings for a sail shade, it's important to get expert advice on installing it. A sail shade shouldn't be attached to a tree if the trunk is less than 250mm in diameter. And if you're attaching a sail to the front of your house, it will need extra support if your walls have cladding.

YOUR NOTES

Gazebo, pergola and arch ideas.

CHAPTER 7
CLIMBING PLANTS

Which plants to grow up your arch, trellis or gazebo? You can even use climbing plants to create a hedge, provided that you give them a good structure to support them, such as a wire frame. You can also disguise a shed by growing climbing plants up the walls.

ANNUALS OR PERENNIALS, DECIDUOUS OR EVERGREEN?

Annuals, such as sweet peas and runner beans, will only cover an arch or trellis in summer, but they will be light. Perennials, such as Hop (*Humulus lupulus*) will climb and

twine around an arch going from nothing to 5 metres in just a few months before dying down again for winter. Other deciduous or semi-evergreen climbers, such as some honeysuckles, clematis and roses, will also lose their leaves in winter, so you won't get as much privacy then. But they are very pretty in summer.

It's also important to note whether your arch, trellis or gazebo is in a largely sunny spot or mainly in the shade. Check plant labels for whether it grows in sun, semi-shade or shade.

And it will also take a climber a few years to get established and to give you the privacy you want. So don't expect full coverage in the first two years.

If you are walking or sitting under an arch regularly, then avoid prickly climbers.

DO YOU WANT YEAR-ROUND COVER FOR PRIVACY?

If so, choose an evergreen climber for your arch or trellis. Check how big the climber is likely to get, because a very dense, heavy clump of climber could bring down an arch or trellis when it's windy unless you keep it properly clipped to shape. If you want to grow the more vigorous climbers, then make sure your wooden arch or trellis is strong and is well secured at its base.

EVERGREEN CLIMBING PLANTS FOR HEDGES

Good evergreen climbers include Clematis armandii (and a few other clematis), many different kinds of Ivy (Hedera), and Star Jasmine (Trachelospermum jasminoides). Honeysuckle (Lonicera) is also a good climber, and there are several semi-evergreen types.

Clematis *armandii* and Clematis *cirrhosa*.

Most clematis aren't evergreen but these two species are vigorous evergreen climbers for a fence, trellis, arbour or pergola. They don't 'share' well with other plants – if you have other climbers on the same structure, the clematis' evergreen leaves and fast growth may strangle the less powerful climbers. They have pretty flowers, some of which are scented.

Ivy (*Hedera helix*).

Ivy is fast-growing and good for wildlife. It's an excellent screen for pollution as it acts as a pollution 'sink', absorbing some of the air pollution from traffic. It's a good option for training up a steel fence, as it will cover it relatively quickly. Some companies now sell 'ivy screens'. An ivy screen is a steel frame which is installed as a screen, windbreak or fence and is then planted with a number of ivy plants.

There are several different kinds of ivy, including ones that do well in coastal areas. In the UK, you can usually grow ivy up to 2.2m without applying for planning permission, although you should check that no special rules apply to where you are planting it.

Star Jasmine (*Trachelospermum jasminoides*).
This is a beautiful trailing plant suitably for training up walls, fences and frames. However it is only hardy in fairly mild climates (USA hardiness zones 8-10, Southern UK and milder parts of Northern Europe or Southern Australia). It's also slow to get established although once it's established it grows more quickly. It has beautiful white flowers with a lovely scent.

Honeysuckle (*Lonicera japonica*).
There are many different honeysuckle variants. They are semi-evergreen, so will lose some leaves, especially in harsh winters. But they are tough, in spite of their pretty, delicate flowers. 'Halliana' is particularly resilient, has two-tone flowers and is happy in semi-shade.

ROSES FOR ARCHES AND TRELLIS

When choosing roses, check whether they prefer sun or will do well in shade. Roses for arches and trellis are divided into climbing and rambling roses. Rambling roses have a sprawling shape and will give lots of cover over an arch but can be quite dense. Some rambling roses, such as 'Kiftsgate' are very vigorous indeed, so you will have to clip them back regularly or make sure that your arch, trellis or pagoda is strong enough to take the weight. Climbing roses have fewer stems, are less dense and will need to be tied in.

It's a good idea to visit a rose nursery so you can see what the rose looks like when it is in full flower. If you can't do that, most rose nurseries will give you advice online or on the phone – it's really worth consulting them to help choose the right rose for your situation.

It will take a climbing or rambling rose a few years to provide cover.

If you are creating a 'secret garden' or sanctuary, think about the fragrance that climbing roses can offer. Look for one with a good scent.

DRAMATIC CLIMBING PLANTS

An arch, arched walkway, trellis or gazebo draped with white or lilac wisteria (*Wisteria sinensis*) will look stunning in May when the wisteria flowers. Passion flower (*Passiflora cerulea*) is also a beautiful climber. Both are deciduous so will lose their leaves in winter.

COMBINING CLIMBERS

It may be tempting to combine a number of climbers on the same trellis, arbour or arch. The idea is that you can benefit because they flower at different times.

But it gets complicated when the plants mature. If you have one climber that doesn't need much pruning intertwined with a clematis that needs cutting to the ground every autumn, then it can be difficult to disentangle the two at pruning time. And climbers that need early pruning can get tangled with those that need late pruning. If you cut a chunk back all at once, you will lose the flowers from one of them.

However a series of arches, such as in a walkway, can help keep climbers a bit more separate so you may be able to get the benefit of different flowering seasons without the climbers getting too entwined.

YOUR NOTES

Climbing plant ideas.

CHAPTER 8
FRONT GARDENS

Front gardens are more likely to have planning limitations than back gardens. In some roads or areas, there are even restrictions on what colour you can paint your front door.

High hedges, fences and walls will give you privacy but they will make your front rooms darker. If you have a long front garden, this is less of a problem. But most front areas are quite small and close to the house.

Traditionally, most front-of-house privacy is achieved through window treatments. These include a lace or net curtain, slatted and venetian blinds or translucent white blind that lets in the maximum light while preventing people from seeing in. But plants and trees can also play a huge part in front garden privacy, and they are so important to the environment. Many leaves help

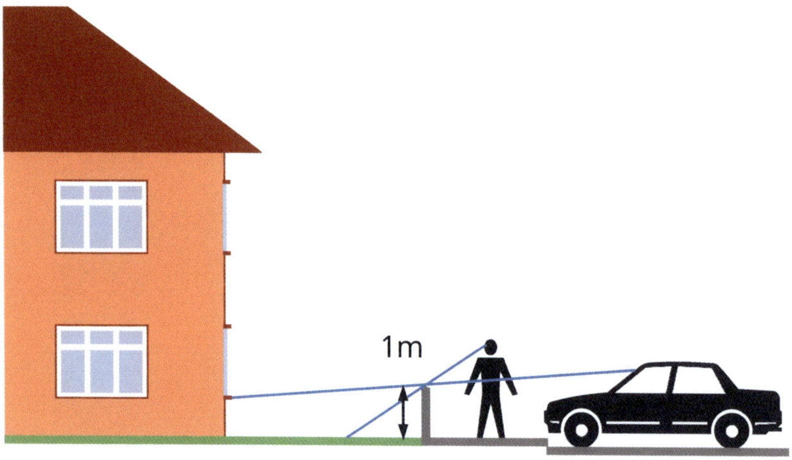

Typical Front Garden Visibility

absorb pollution and improve oxygen levels in the air. Paved over front gardens lead to problems with run-off and flash flooding, and they also affect the health of earthworms. Even if you need your front garden space for parking, look at where you can make it more permeable, more green and more private.

THINK ABOUT THE EYELINE

Front garden privacy need be no higher than the eyeline height of a passer-by. Shrubs or plants that are 6ft tall from the pavement will stop almost everyone from seeing into your rooms. And they don't need to be an absolutely solid screen. You can effectively distract the eye with an attractive mixed planting, even if you can technically see through some of it.

WINDOW BOXES FOR PRIVACY

If your windows to the street are quite high off the ground, then a window box may be all you need to increase your privacy inside your front rooms.

It's important to make sure that the window box is well secured to the window sill. If it falls off in a high wind, it could hurt someone or damage property.

It's also essential to buy a window box that has some kind of water reservoir. There are a number of these on the market.
A water reservoir means that if you can't get to water your window box, then the plants can take up water from the reservoir, which is an area just below the roots. But, more importantly, it's also your first line of defence against over-watering. If water just dribbles straight through the window box and down the front of your house, it can damage paintwork.

If you want an old-fashioned look to your window box – for example, you want a painted wooden one – then you could have one made. Then put the resin or plastic window box with a reservoir inside the wooden shell. The top

style tip for planting window boxes is to keep to only two or three colours. Your green foliage is one colour! So either add one or two colours to that.

If you want a window box for privacy, you'll want plants that add height. It's likely that you'll want to re-plant the window box at least twice a year for summer and winter choices. And check whether your window box is mainly sunny or mainly shady, and choose plants appropriately.

Good choices include easy-care plants like pelargoniums. Herbs, such as rosemary and sage, are relatively easy to look after and you'll be able to use them in cooking. You can choose an all-foliage scheme, using variegated leaves such as coleus and architecturally shaped leaves like ferns.

Most plants will grow in a pot or window box for one season at least. So you don't necessarily need to stick to plants recommended for window boxes, provided that you check whether they want a sunny or shady spot and how high they grow.

RAISED BEDS AND POTS FOR FRONT GARDEN PRIVACY

Raised beds are often consigned to the vegetable patch, but they are easy to look after. If you build a raised bed in your front garden, then you raise the planting too.
If your raised bed is, for example, 2-3ft high, you have a huge choice of plants that grow to around 3ft, making a total of six foot high. You can enjoy a splash of colour from your windows and passers-by won't be able to see in so easily.
A wooden raised bed and bin store combination would give you a co-ordinated way of concealing bins, too.
Large planters with tall plants in them can also create more privacy. Consider bamboos, which grow tall. Small trees, such as fruit trees, will also grow in planters. However, planters will need to be carefully secured as front garden pots are more vulnerable to theft.

Raised beds in a front garden have replaced the hedge or fence, but there is still room for a parking area. Designed by Professor David Stephens for BBC Gardeners World Live.

This tiny front garden, designed by Posy Gentles (posygentles.co.uk) uses three elements. There is a low wall, a slightly higher privet hedge and tall, airy plants behind that.

SHRUBS, HEDGES AND TREES

A hedge is always a popular front garden choice, and there is a list of good evergreen hedging in Chapter 3. Be aware that a fast-growing hedge, such as privet, will get to the height you want quite quickly, but after that you will need to clip it two or three times a year. A slow-growing hedge, such as yew, will probably only need a once-a-year clip, but it may take five years or more to get to the height you want. Large shrubs and small trees are also good choices. Look at our list of tree shapes in Chapter 4 to decide what shape tree you would like. For example, if you want a little more privacy for an upper front window, but are short of space on the ground, then choose a vase-shaped tree, such as Ornamental Pear.

Trees and shrubs can be evergreen or deciduous, so check which you are buying. You may not need year-round privacy, but if you do, you will need to choose evergreen plants.

Most shrubs have a number of varieties, some of which may not get tall enough to increase your front garden privacy. Check the botanical name and the variety (see our "TIP: Check your plant names!" explanation in Chapter 1). For example, most viburnums reach around 2.5 metres, which is an excellent height for a shrub for privacy. But *Viburnum juddii* will only reach 1-1.5m. Some hydrangeas, such as the popular 'Limelight', will reach 2.5m, but many others will only be 1m tall.

If you have a solid evergreen hedge, wall or fence, be aware of security issues in your front garden. Could someone hide in there without being spotted?

YOUR NOTES

Jot down the places of front gardens you particularly like, or sketch their outlines here.

CHAPTER 9
EYESORES

Whether you live in a city, town or the countryside, there are always things you'd rather not see. Service stations, windfarms, tower blocks, garage roofs, street lamps, air conditioning units (especially other people's!) and advertising billboards are common eyesores.

But the most complaints come when neighbours build an extension. Even if they take the greatest care with the design and the materials, and even if there are no overlooking windows, a new extension or garden building feels like an intrusion, especially in the first few years.

There may also be smaller eyesores in your own garden, such as an ugly pipe, drain or refuse bins. You may not want to look at your compost heaps or plastic water butt. And although sheds can be beautiful, they can also be ugly. A lick of paint may be all you need to transform your shed from eyesore to charming.

TO BLOCK OR TO DISTRACT?

There are three ways of reducing the impact of an eyesore. One option is to block it – to cover it with a tree, screen or hedge. Smaller eyesores, such as bins and pipes, can almost always be covered up or planted over. Just make sure you have easy access for when you need it.

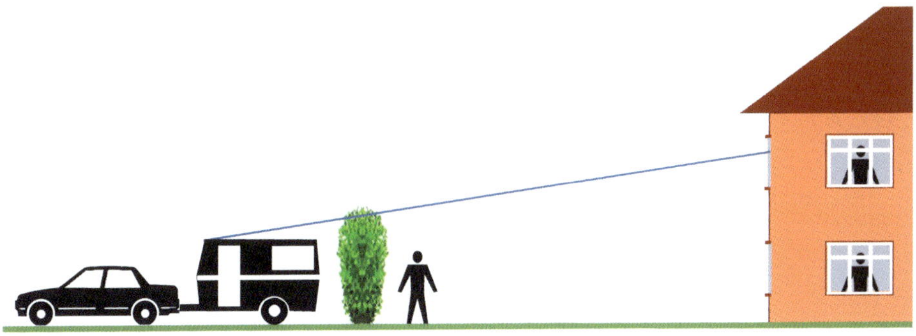

Eyesore 1 – Neighbour Caravan

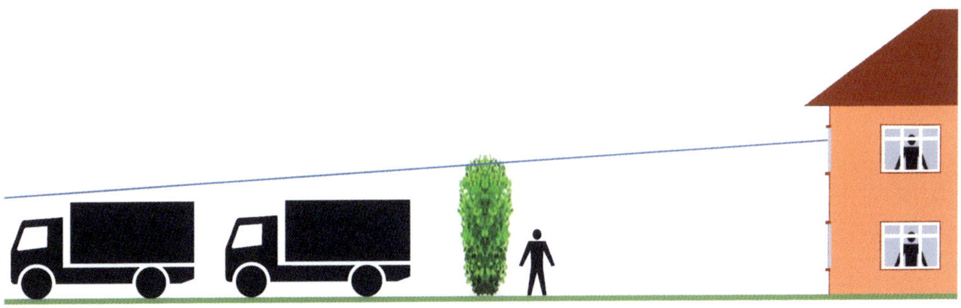

Eyesore 2 – Lorry Park

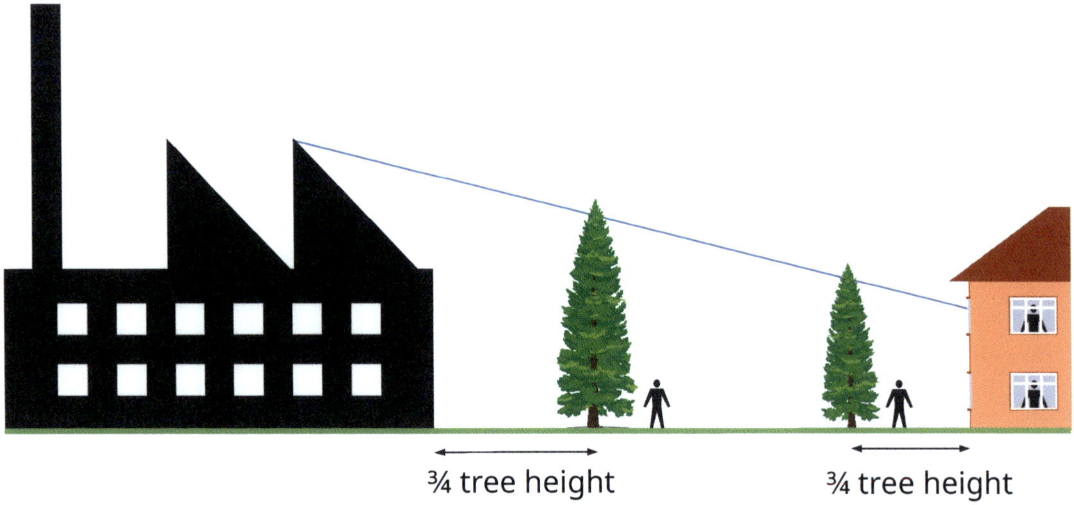

Eyesore 3 – Industrial

Something tall but narrow, such as a street lamp, can often be hidden by a single tree. See chapter 4 for suitable tree shapes and recommendations for trees for privacy.

But check the sightline before deciding where to plant the tree. You may not be able to cover all the light from the streetlamp, so place the tree where it will block the sight line you really care about. If you don't want the light to invade a bedroom window for example, plant the tree in the line between the street light and the window. But be aware that your tree's branches must stay within your property – you can't allow foliage to obscure the street lamp or signage for other road users.

However, it's unlikely that you will be able to cover up a large building unless you also have a very large garden and can plant a number of trees between you and the object you want to disguise.

If you do have a large garden, don't plant a row of trees at the end in order to cover the building. A row of trees in a line draws attention to that part of the garden. And by the time the trees are tall enough to conceal the eyesore, they will cast a great deal of shade into your garden.

Instead, stagger a number of trees at different points around the garden, choosing some for autumn foliage and spring blossom, and others for evergreen coverage. Take pleasure in designing a really attractive scheme with as many trees as you feel comfortable with, remembering that the deciduous trees will lose their leaves in winter, so you may have to look at the building or extension if you are outside in winter.

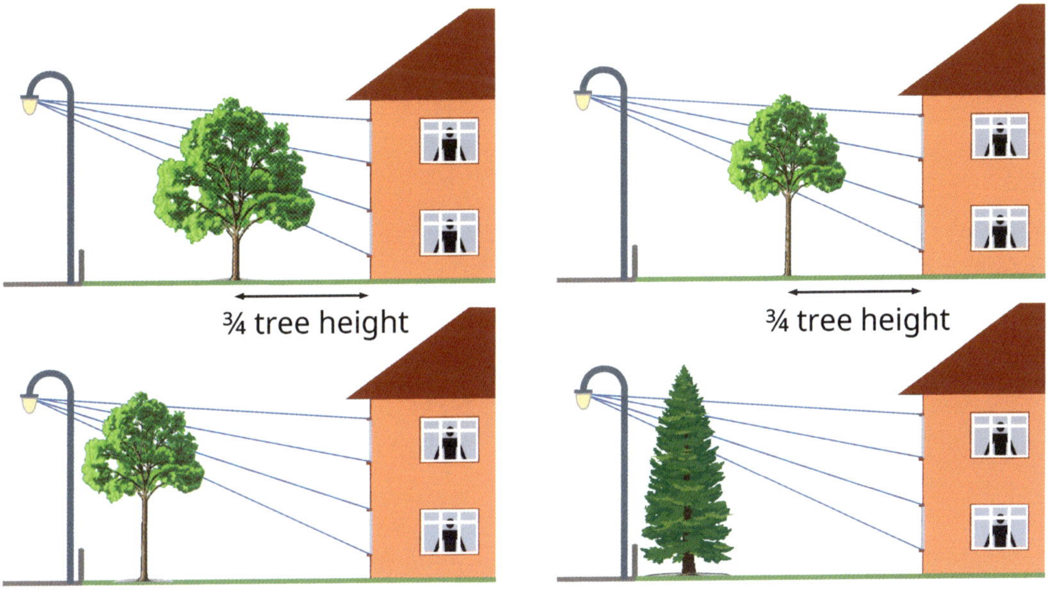

Options for a Front Garden Tree

DISTRACT THE EYE

The second option is to reduce the impact of the eyesore rather than block it completely. Distract the eye so you're less aware of it. If you have a beautiful tree, arch, sculpture or feature as a focal point in your garden, then that is where the eye will look.

You could also create a seating area or areas that don't face the eyesore. Reverse engineer the principles of primary and secondary space in chapter 1. A low ornamental screen near a table not only blocks a view of people sitting at that table – it also prevents those who are sitting down from seeing an eyesore.

Make one part of the garden into a special area where you can't see the eyesore, using the principles in this book. Combine a screen, a tree and a gazebo to make a private 'secret garden'.

This attractive eating area by garden designer Kate Gould is protected by an artistic trellis behind it. Look at the chairs and tables. Do you notice the tents behind? Now focus on the tents. You can see them, but you don't notice them when you're enjoying the area. An excellent example of distracting the eye.

COME TO TERMS WITH THE EYESORE

The third option is to come to terms with the eyesore. This may seem impossible at first. It can be very distressing to be forced to look at something new which you don't personally like. However, three or four years later, you may hardly notice it. If a neighbour's extension doesn't have over-looking windows, it may actually increase your privacy, too.

If you are the one thinking of building an extension, remember that however beautifully you do it, the neighbours are unlikely to like it. The more you can engage with them about what their real concerns are, the less likely you are to fall out with them.

SECURITY LIGHTS

A final eyesore – the neighbour's security light. You might like this for your own security, but usually it's an inconvenience. Even if it's only on occasionally and briefly, a sudden harsh light turning on can disturb a social event or contemplative moment.

Use the principles in this book to interrupt the glare of the security light, so it doesn't shine in your eyes when you're sitting outside, for example. Think about the line of the light and where you will be when you are most disturbed by it.

The Security Light

YOUR NOTES

Make notes on eyesores you may wish to disguise.

CHAPTER 10
NOISE AND WIND

It's harder to screen out noise than it is to interrupt a line of sight. You may have been told that the sound of a water feature or wind chimes will block the sound of your neighbours partying in their jacuzzi. It won't. But there are ways you can soften the impact of neighbouring noise to some extent.

NOISE GOES FURTHER ON THE WIND

Have you ever been sitting in your garden and suddenly noticed that the traffic noise seems much greater than usual? Then a few days later, you hardly can hear it?

That's because the wind carries the noise further. Perhaps you have a major road around a mile away. When the wind is blowing strongly, particularly in your direction, the traffic noise seems quite loud. At other times, there is little wind or its direction has changed. Your garden seems free of road noise.

So that means that a windbreak will reduce noise – up to a point. Noise doesn't just travel in a single straight line. It takes many paths. A windbreak can block and filter some noise, but some will simply travel around the barrier.

If you live a mile away from a busy road, then there will be houses, hedges and trees in between. They will absorb or deflect some of the traffic noise. But not all. Some noise will travel over the houses, especially in a strong wind.

So while a windbreak will reduce the noise you hear, it won't get rid of it entirely.

WILL A HEDGE SOFTEN NOISE AND WIND MORE THAN A FENCE OR A WALL?

Research (by the National Agroforestry Center of the US Forest Service, part of the US Department of Agriculture) has been carried out into windbreaks, and how hedges, fences and walls compare.

We have checked this research and it looks very reliable. However, it has been done on farms, where the distances involved are huge compared to a domestic garden.

The research says that a hedge will filter the wind, reducing its strength for a distance several times the height of the hedge. But when wind hits a solid barrier, such as a fence or a wall, although its stops completely at the barrier itself, it rises up and lands on the other side, still windy and creating eddies. So is a hedge a better windbreak than a solid barrier?

The diagrams below show wind direction and strength. The longer the arrow the stronger the wind. The short arrows show where the wind is weakest.

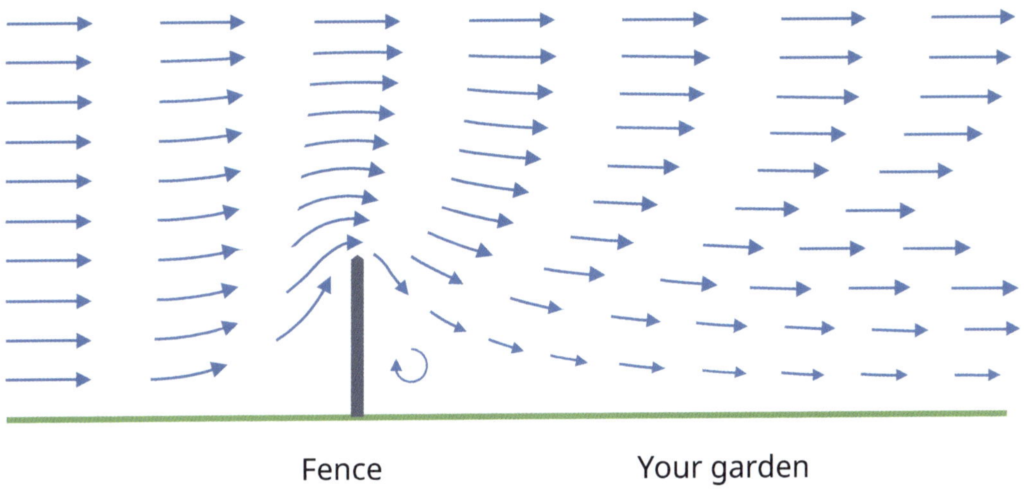

Wind direction and strength over a fence or wall. The longer the arrow the stronger the wind.

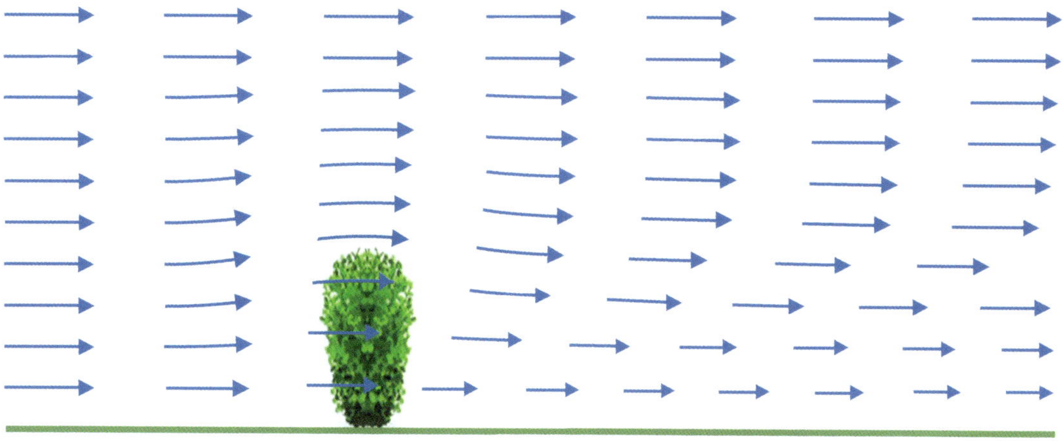

Wind direction and strength over and through a hedge

There are lots of factors. A barrier's height, density, orientation, length, width and continuity all affect the profile of the wind. As a general rule, a high-density hedge (such as a conifer) gives more wind protection for a distance that is more than five times the height of the windbreak. In large gardens and farmland, you need a windbreak that is still effective 10, 20 or even 50 metres away from the barrier.

In a domestic garden, which may typically be 10 metres wide, the decision is different. The filtered wind from a hedge gives more shelter over the longer distances, but in small areas a solid break gives more shelter.

The key measurements from the research are shown as a graph on the opposite page.

WHEN A WALL OR FENCE IS BETTER

If you have a solid windbreak, then there is a small area on both sides of it that will be completely free of wind. The wind then gets stronger further away and, at a distance about five times the height of the windbreak, exceeds the wind going through a high-density hedge. So if you have a 2 metre (6ft) fence or wall, then it will be a relatively effective windbreak for up to 10 metres or about 30ft away from it.

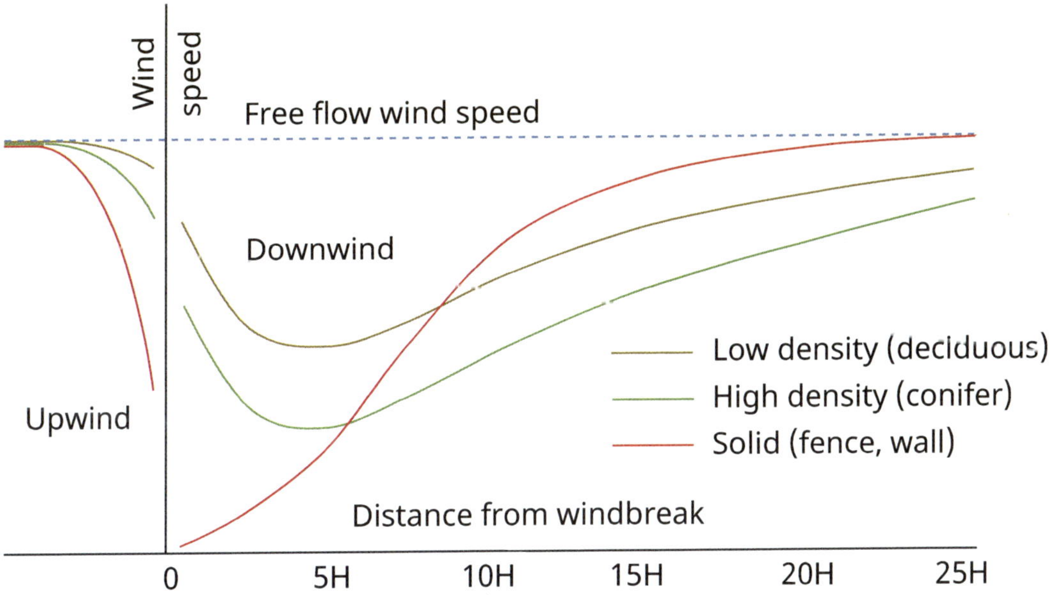

Graph of wind speed versus distance from the windbreak

That's enough to create a sheltered area in most domestic gardens. Beyond that, a high-density hedge is more effective.

A low-density hedge (eg deciduous) becomes more effective beyond 8-10 times the height.

BUT A HEDGE DOES MORE...

With a hedge, you'll always have some wind, no matter how close you are to the hedge. However, it's not just noise that is carried on the wind. It's also pollution particulates, pollen, smell, ozone and carbon monoxide. Hedges absorb pollution and carbon monoxide, so they make a good choice for front gardens.

If you have industrial or farmyard smells locally, then a wind barrier will reduce those smells, too. Once again, it won't get rid of them. But you may want to consider planting more hedges and trees between you and the source of the smell.

Remember that smells, pollution particulates etc are carried on the wind. So the filtering effect of a hedge or other barrier is only as high as the hedge. Some of the wind, with the smells, pollution etc goes straight over it.

A DENSE BARRIER ABSORBS MORE NOISE

A thick wall, built two bricks deep, will absorb more noise than a fence that is one single thickness of board.

A hedge is less dense than both so if it is at all gappy, it will let more noise through.

It's very expensive to build a wall, however. You can get some extra protection with acoustic fencing, which is designed to baffle sound. This works better in bigger spaces (ie between you and a busy road). It's not really designed to buffer sound between neighbours in small gardens.

You would need several rows of shrubs and trees to significantly reduce neighbouring noise. However, if you plant a hedge in front of the fence, that will reduce the noise a little more than just having the fence on its own.

WHY REDUCING NOISE HELPS

The human ear hates sudden, loud noises. We adjust fairly well over time to steady background noise. So reducing the level of any noise always helps bring the overall level of noise down to something we can get used to.

The more you think about something, the more you will notice it. So it is worth practicing acceptance of the fact that your neighbour spends two hours a week mowing his lawn or chain-sawing logs. It can help to enjoy music or a podcast on your mobile phone through earphones.

FIND OUT WHERE THE PREVAILING WIND COMES FROM

It's important to know where the wind generally comes from before protecting yourself from it. You will have a local prevailing wind, a dominant direction, but at any one time it will vary to one side or the other. So the windbreak needs to extend beyond. A small garden with fences, walls or hedges all round it should feel quite sheltered, but you can often get even more protection by planting taller trees and shrubs between you and the prevailing wind.

HOW TO MAKE A 'SECRET GARDEN' LESS NOISY

A garden with a lawn and lots of plants will have fewer echoes than one which has hard landscaping like stone paving, brick walls and minimalist planting. It's like having bare boards or limestone floors inside a house. You will be able to hear people's footsteps and the clatter of furniture moving. Once again, however, the difference may not be very great. It's just worth considering.

So if you're creating a part of the garden as a sanctuary or secret garden, remember that hard landscaping materials may feel more noisy. Green, soft planting and a tiny patch of lawn will smell and feel fresh and clean.

YOUR NOTES

Make notes on reducing noise.

APPENDIX: MY GARDEN PRIVACY PLANNER

Part 1. Issues

			An issue? Y/N	OK, so what are the details? (separate sheet if required)
My visibility problems	Looking in	Neighbours		
		Public (pedestrians, vehicles)		
	Looking out	Eyesores		
		Streetlamps, security lights		
My garden	Shape			
	Boundaries			
My privacy areas	Primary			
	Secondary			
My sightline targets	From where, to where, and what area			
Further considerations	Seasonal - all year or summer only			
	Growth speed - how many years to mature			
	Noise - type, direction			
	Wind - prevailng direction			
	Physical security - a worry?			
Constraints	Ground infrastructure - pipes, cabling			
	Regulations - national, local			
	Timescale - to set it up			
	Resources - yours, others			
	Budget - how much you can afford			

APPENDIX: MY GARDEN PRIVACY PLANNER

Part 2. Solutions

		Solution? Y/N	OK, so what are the details? (separate sheet if required)
Walls and fences	Existing, potential		
	Positions, shapes, dimensions		
	Suitable types		
	Your choice(s)		
Hedges	Existing, potential		
	Positions, shapes, dimensions		
	Suitable types		
	Your choice(s)		
Trees	Existing, potential		
	Positions, shapes, dimensions		
	Suitable types		
	Your choice(s)		
Screens	Existing, potential		
	Positions, shapes, dimensions		
	Suitable types		
	Your choice(s)		
Other structures (see * below)	Existing, potential		
	Positions, shapes, dimensions		
	Suitable types		
	Your choice(s)		
Climbing plants	Existing, potential		
	Positions, shapes, dimensions		
	Suitable types		
	Your choice(s)		

* Other structures: sheds, arches, pergolas, arbours, gazebos, parasols/sails, window boxes, raised beds/pots, shrubs.

APPENDIX: MY GARDEN PRIVACY PLANNER

Part 3. Planning	Planned? Y/N	OK, so what are the details? (separate sheet if required)
Phasing & timescales		
Detailed action list		
Costs		

Printed in Great Britain
by Amazon

59114823R00061